Waking Up Dead: A Loose Collection of Anecdotes from Life as the Son of a Funeral Director and Coroner, Among Other Things.

By Ryan Copeland

© 2020

Rebecca —
I hope you (and your Son)
I enjoy!

TABLE OF CONTENTS

Preface

History always points to the ancient Egyptians as being the first to embalm or preserve bodies, and thus they're generally called the pioneers of funeral directing. Morticians, undertakers, gravediggers...they're all the same and they've all worn dark suits and pale faces since King Tutankhamen was a young lad.

Even before the Egyptians, however, you have to imagine that someone was designated to take care of the deceased.

Cavemen, for example, probably didn't just let Bob and his wife Susanne lie there in the open brush not breathing. Someone had to take care of the bodies after the terrible bear-wrestling incident.

And so, gathered around a campfire at their nightly Neanderthal gathering, Larry drew the short rock and was tasked with getting rid of the bodies. Whether he threw them on the fire and yelled with enthusiasm as the flames rose or simply buried them in a shallow sandlot he dug with his hands, we'll never know.

But he did such a good job with it, and with comforting young Bob, Jr. and Jessica Denise, that when they needed someone to investigate what happened to Elder MacGinty when his lips turned blue and he fell over mid-sentence, Larry was elected to determine that cause of death, too. Poor guy didn't even have time to draw the short rock.

Several thousand years later, my dad was thrust into the same position - funeral director and Coroner for nearly 30 years in a small(ish) town on the coast of South Carolina. His caseload in that time increased with the advancing years at a rate similar to the plaque buildup in his arteries, and he landed himself in the news quite often, usually as an authority figure but also sometimes as an agitant.

Growing up I was always asked if I lived at the morgue. Does a professional baseball player's family live in the dugout? There's a natural curiosity for the rare things around us, and perhaps it leads sometimes to ignorant inferences. Even now, though, people call me "morbid," even if I prefer "absurdist." I suppose my experiences in life and my outlook would have been quite different had my dad been a pharmacist or an auto mechanic. I might have fascinating tales of moving pills from the big bottle to the smaller bottle or that lug nut wrench that just wouldn't crank anymore.

As it is, I can only write about his experiences from my perspective and memory. He is no longer around to give it firsthand, but the following is what I can remember best from some of his years practicing what the Ancient Egyptians - or cavemen - practiced long before him.

This started, for me, as an attempt to recall certain encounters I had. I told a humorously grotesque story to my family about falling into a grave as a child. It was a story I had forgotten or maybe purposely put deep into the recesses of my mind as it didn't reflect well on my decision-making. When I was six or seven years old I saw an open grave in the cemetery at my dad's funeral home and thought it would be fun to jump down into it. It would be easier to explain casually falling into it or even being pushed by a malevolent force, but I was the idiot who jumped. I yelled for help and, after several seconds of hearing no reply, made my peace with the fact that I would die in a grave already meant for someone else. It was then that I looked up into a face that temporarily blocked the sun, and the man who reached his hand down into the grave smiled at me before rescuing me.

He worked for my dad at the time and for several years after, so when I saw him out and about in town recently after not having seen him for years, it spurred the memory.

My eldest niece, the one of his grandchildren who probably remembers him best, asked me to write down more stories about their "GDaddy."

I don't know everything about the funeral business, I can only report my observations. My dad packed a lot of living into 65 years, and most of those adult years were spent with the dead and their surviving loved ones. This is not an attempt to right any wrongs through an unrealistic hagiography or produce some kind of "warts and all" biography. It's just setting out the things I personally found amusing. Many of you won't, and that's okay too.

These are stories and experiences that are unique to me, as the child of a funeral director and coroner, yes, but also unique in the entirety of the American experience. It's an amalgam of incidents from my own perspective. Few have been born into the funeral business, as incongruous as that sounds. Fewer still were raised in it, handed it to them on a silver platter and flat-out refused in the kindest way acceptable.

I hope you enjoy these memories. If not, I'll be at the morgue.

CHAPTER I.

Some things you remember well, especially if it's the first time you experience them. You can usually remember the first time you tried to kiss a girl and it was awkward because she wasn't expecting it and she hit you on the arm for being weird. You can remember the first time you got out on a baseball field and the coach told you to play "backup to First Base," which is a totally made up position. You remember the first time your boat got stuck on a sandbar and someone in a much smaller boat kindly towed you away with everyone watching. Things like that never leave you.

Unfortunately, neither does the experience of your first time in an embalming room.

I was 9, and for whatever reason my mom had taken me to see my dad at work.

I kind of had a good idea what he did for a living, don't get me wrong, but until you see it in action you just kind of have to guess.

When you first walked into Copeland Funeral Home back then, the front doors opened into a sitting area on the left and a small assistant's desk inside a small, glass-doored office on the right. Just past the assistant's desk to the right was a hallway. Down that hallway on the left was the casket display room. Across the hall from the casket room was my dad's office, which included a nice view of the highway out front.

All of the halls and rooms and offices included high ceilings and pastel colored-walls. Dad didn't want the place to feel dark and grim and closing in on you while you're already in a vulnerable position coming to a place that some people dread.

Back to the left of the main entrance hall were two viewing rooms where the visitations took place, what old-timers and people from above Mason-Dixon might call a wake. Just beyond those two rooms was the E.C. Copeland Memorial Chapel, named for the grandfather I'd never met. The carpets always seemed vacuumed - so much so that I hated putting my own footprints into them.

Towards the end of the hall - directly at the end, actually - were two doors that could swing open towards you, a very welcoming invitation to the embalming room.

The doors were generally locked, for good reason. Dad hated people wandering around and seeing things they weren't supposed to see. Above the double doors of the embalming room was a clear "Personnel Only - Do Not Enter" sign. For some that's just an invitation to tomfoolery, but for most it can only mean "this is the room where the stuff happens that you don't want to see."

On this particular day, it was also where my dad happened to be working.

Outside the doors of doom, I asked my mom why we were clearly headed in there.

"This is where your dad is working today."

Putting two and two together I asked if there would be bones, i.e. skeletal remains. Yes, I was a dumb kid. You'd think I'd have known by then.

"No, honey. Not at all," she said as she slowly opened the door on the right.

I could feel her watching me as I peeked around the corner of the door, leaving all but my head and neck still squarely in the hall. "My sweet little dum-dum," she probably thought. It was obvious she was showing me my dad at work but the reason didn't hit me until I saw the person lying on the table.

His hair, gently being washed and rinsed by my dad, was longer and darker than mine. A thin, white, wet sheet covered him up to just below his shoulders. His face was youthful, now eternally so. It was almost angelic, though it's strange to think that way of a boy only three years older than me at the time. His skin was pale but truly seemed to be glowing.

I saw my dad look up and say hello as if he were simply watering a fern. Around him in this white-walled room were various bottles of chemicals and hoses and sinks. He had on a white nylon apron and was chewing gum, a sure sign of nervousness for someone who usually went outside to discreetly light a cigarette in those cases.

He was nervous, I was later to learn, because he didn't do a ton of embalming anymore. He had two other licensed embalmers on staff, but in certain cases he felt a need to do a more personal job, especially when the deceased was a member of a personal family friend.

My mom stood behind me and probably said something to my dad, but my eyes were too transfixed on Angel Boy to look anywhere else. There no were no flutterings of his eyelids or slight heaves in his chest. He was as still as time was for me while I looked.

I heard my dad tell my mom he'd be finished and out in a few minutes. I walked back out the door and into his office with my mom to wait.

It was there, in his office in those same leather, low-back chairs that countless other families had sat in to discuss uncomfortable subjects, that my mom told me about Angel Boy.

Up until a couple of days before he certainly had been just a normal young teenager. He'd probably been out on his bike in the last week, riding the same kind of dirt roads that I liked, popping wheelies over potholes and feeling the sweat trickle down his back. It was summer, and all boys my age seemed to love summer.

Only this boy, we'll now call him RJ, had been playing with another neighborhood friend when they decided to go inside the house and open up RJ's dad's gun closet. He and the neighborhood kid, one who was my age and in my grade in school, had no idea the gun was loaded. Either they just didn't know how to check the chamber or they were simply neglectful, it's hard to say and it didn't matter now. They were just kids.

Until they weren't.

"Is this how you shoot it?" the friend probably asked as he aimed it at RJ.

Before RJ could answer, a bullet hit him at close range and the lives of the neighborhood friend and his family, not to mention RJ's family, were changed forever. These were two boys from two prominent and well-adjusted families, proving that when a gun fires accidentally, it doesn't take socio-economic status into account.

To her credit, in later years RJ's mother tirelessly dedicated herself to trying to pass legislation in South Carolina, specifically the Children's Firearm Protection Act, to help prevent a death that was certainly preventable.

Why it was important for me to not only hear the story of what happened but also see the result wasn't really clear to me at the time.

I've never really messed around with guns since that time, I can tell you that, and I know that my dad never really tried to bring his work home, but something in that situation disturbed him enough to bring me to his work.

What apparently didn't disturb him was sometimes leaving his paperwork at home.

As easily as I can recall seeing RJ's body under that sheet in the embalming room, I can remember the time I saw a stack of photos sitting on the roll-top desk in our living room at home. My mom, in her prime, must have taken a roll of film a week, leading to rows and rows of family photo albums. I enjoyed looking through the captured moments, for sure.

Only, this particular roll inside the Revco processing packaging was not my mom's.

The first picture I pulled out was of a woman, clearly deceased and clearly not in any familiar pose. It was easy to tell from the blood that had pooled around her and the unnatural positions her limbs were in.

I took the entire roll to my mom, next door in the kitchen, for an explanation.

"Mom, why were you taking pictures of..."

Before I could finish, she grabbed the stack from me.

It hadn't hit me that they were my dad's roll. Did I not mention I was dumb?

She walked off quickly towards her bedroom, mumbling under her breath about "your father" and "cannot believe" and some other unfamiliar words.

It started to dawn on me that him taking pictures like this must have been part of his job, and it must have been an unpleasant part. He did talk to me later that evening, explaining that the woman had died in a car accident and he needed it for evidence because the accident was not the woman's fault but that of another driver. He was sorry I'd seen it, but he'd had it developed and picked up in a rush and left it mistakenly on the desk.

The photo will never leave me. What struck me was how average the woman seemed. There was nothing about her, even in death, that was out-of-place or unbelievable. Her hair was cut in a modern fashion. Her dress and shoes matched, both a shade of teal. She looked, in fact, like someone my mom would be friends with, and she probably was someone's mom. Or at least she used to be until she took a turn down a road at the same time as someone who shouldn't have been there.

Of course it was only a couple of years later that a similar photo resurfaced at my elementary school.

Career Day is always great when you get to hear from a classmate whose dad is, let's say, a firefighter who runs with blazing speed into a burning building. Or maybe one of your classmates has a mom who is a nurse, and you can almost feel the pulse of the heart she's massaging back into rhythm as she recounts the story of her emergency room bravery.

But suddenly the lights in the cafeteria go down and a projector screen comes out. Popcorn! Reel-to-reel films! Walt Disney!

But it's none of those things. It's your dad, with a microphone.

"Good morning, boys and girls!" he says, and you can't slide down your seat fast enough. "I wanted to take a few minutes to talk to you about the importance of wearing your seatbelt..."

Out came picture after picture of car accidents. Minivans crushed to random scraps of metal. Motorcycles wrapped around trees. The backs of EMS workers with the familiar Star of Life logo lifting stretchers with fully-covered sheets into the ambulance. The kids in the cafeteria wouldn't so much gasp as scream, the way kids presented with blood and gore at 8:30 in the morning would do.

"Let's talk just for a few minutes about death and dying!" he'd say, to the applause of no one.

The photos were so iconic that kids at my school would talk about it years later, bringing up its impact.

"Remember those slide shows your dad would do?" they'd say, as if he were a juggling clown who showed up at the world's saddest birthday parties.

"That shit messed me up for years!"

But maybe it also saved lives. Dad was an early crusader for seat belts at a time when they were considered optional, and every newspaper editorial or 6:00 newscast he could press the issue into, he would.

"I've never taken a seat belt off a dead person," he'd say.

He'd been on the seatbelt crusade for years at that point. It may have started when I was two years old, or at least what happened then could have contributed to his dedication to seatbelt safety.

As on most mornings, my dad had gone out and started my mom's car for her in preparation for her taking me to daycare on her way to her job teaching at Battery Creek High School. The neighbor's child, four year-old Katy, also rode with us because she and I attended the same daycare.

My dad, as he always did, took my sister, Shelley, to elementary school on the other side of town on his own way to work. My sister, six years older than me and very much a mother hen, had just helped me get into my car seat in the back of the car. My parents were still inside the house getting ready while the cars warmed up. Engines back in those days took forever. Actually I don't know that they did; I'm just assuming since it was the 1980's everything was a little more lax.

While my sister worked to get me in my car seat, Katy climbed into the front of the car in an attempt to get to the passenger side. To get leverage in moving across the front seat, she grabbed the shifting column over the steering wheel. Predictably, it shifted the car into gear and sent the car careening forward into the garage door. My sister screamed and grabbed me and pulled me out of the backseat. Katy screamed and continued to drive towards the garage.

As my dad came running out because of the commotion, the car hit the garage door. He managed to jump in and hit the brakes in time to stop it from going on into the kitchen. My sister watched as my car seat fell face-forward onto the pavement from the still-open back door. Her crying became sobbing at that point.

Katy would be fine, though she would go on to run into another garage door, as well as a fence and another car in her teen years. I'm not even making that up for comic effect.

Had I been buckled into the back seat I probably would have been fine too, a point missed by no one else there. My mom went on to take me and Katy to daycare and then to work. She was old-school that way. I don't remember her missing many sick days over her career, and certainly her vehicle slamming into her house wasn't excuse enough to be late to work.

My dad, on the other hand, took my sister down the street to her elementary school after she had calmed down a bit.

Katy's mom, Cindy, also happened to be a teacher at the school. After Dad dropped off Shelley with her first grade class, he went down to Cindy's class.

At that point, the phenomenon of seeing the Coroner in an unexpected place at an unexpected time occurred. Cindy freaked.

As Dad bent down by her desk, he said "first thing you should know is Katy is okay," he said.

"Well spit it out, what happened!?" said Cindy.

Understandably, she was apprehensive about seeing her neighbor, friend and elected County Coroner in her classroom. It happened to Dad a lot over his career, and he never stopped being hurt when people made jokes about seeing him in public and thinking the worst. It's a natural reaction, though, and once he explained that he just didn't want Cindy to hear about it from someone who may have been driving by and seen the damage to the house, she was also okay.

I'm sure that it was interesting having to be a regular human while also walking around as the harbinger of bad news in the community. Cindy herself would ask, just a couple years later, to see what it looked like when someone was embalmed. The day she'd chosen to come out to the funeral home to witness one was on the second half of an embalming double-header. I don't know if that's what it's called in the business so much as I relate everything to baseball, but when she got to the embalming room, she met my dad coming out with tears literally streaming down his face.

He'd just had to embalm a baby, something he almost always did himself without asking someone else to, even if it bothered his sense of humanity immensely.

He always told my mom that "if it ever becomes just a job to me, it's time to get out."

Still, it was a very different calling, even if someone had to do it. As I grew I also started to realize that people saw me as different just by extension of what my dad did for a living.

Yet, as naturally as my sister gravitated towards my dad, I spent more time around my mom growing up. She was the teacher who had summers off to spend with us, and it was generally more fun to play basketball by myself in the gym of Battery Creek High School as a kid than to spend the day trying to decide which casket in the display room was more comfortable.

It doesn't mean I didn't have my fun.

The fourth home I lived in had a basement in the garage, and when I had two friends over one day who asked what was down there I told them it was where we kept the bodies because it was darker and cooler down there.

"You're lying," the smarter of the two said.

"Let's go take a look," said the dummy.

"Here, if you're going down there now take a couple of these with you," I said, reaching for a small paper with string on it my dad used for identifying the roses in his garden.

"Are those toe tags?!" said the brainiac.

"Yep - there's a couple bodies down there right now without them," I said.

They took the tags and then a couple of tentative steps towards the basement door. As soon as they were in a few steps I shut off the lights and closed the door behind them.

They never asked again about my dad bringing work home with him.

Even when he wasn't bringing work home, which in the form of an actual body he never did, he was finding his work even on family vacations. We never went anywhere without visiting a major cemetery (Hollywood Forever in L.A., Arlington National in D.C.) or simply stopping by a funeral home if it was just visible off the interstate. We literally did this more than once - Charlotte, Las Vegas, Boston...they all had funeral homes where my dad would just "pop in" to see how they ran things.

I guess I sort of understand that notion now because I spent hours just casing out the New York Public Library in Manhattan, to the detriment and despair of my wife and kids.

But Dad also went with us to every family funeral we ever attended. In Beaufort, my mom's family alone encompassed my grandparents, my grandmother's three sisters and two brothers, all their children and most of their grandchildren. In addition, most of the rest of my extended family was not far in various places in South Carolina like Greer, Union, Edgefield and Rains. That's a lot of elderly family members who were dying at the rate of basically one or two per year at one point. I'm not going to say Dad got "excited" by funerals, but he definitely kept a watchful eye on the proceedings when he wasn't in charge, ready to jump in and lead a family out of a church pew during a recessional.

My dad was of the opinion that children should be exposed to death at funerals at an early age, so I've been attending them since I could talk. At a service at a Methodist church in Edgefield for one of my mom's uncle's I remember staring at the stained-glass window behind the altar for what felt like hours, secretly hoping Jesus would drop the lamb He was holding and ask the minister to move the service on along.

I didn't realize until later how strange it was to have been at so many funerals by the time I was 20. That doesn't even take into account the times I was asked to be a pallbearer myself for a great-aunt or great-uncle, one of whom was diminutive in stature but had a casket that weighed approximately 2,000 pounds and that I may or may not have started to drop on the way from the church to the graveyard.

I'm not sure if, like my school friends, that "shit" ever messed me up completely, but those early incidents in my own life - seeing the result of what happens when breathing ceases - started to at least give me indication that my dad's job was a little different from others. Most of my friends had dads who were real estate agents and veterinarians and chemists and teachers. The stories they had to tell were generally much less colorful.

CHAPTER II.

What I'd continue to learn in later years was just how much of this funeral business was ingrained in my dad. People always said "it takes someone special" to do that kind of work, as if funeral directors put on overalls to go down into sewers and scavenge for dimes every day. I knew what they meant, though, because there always seemed to be so few funeral directors in any given county. Almost every other profession seemed to have at least a dozen or more people working in it within a given radius.

If you've ever been to a funeral director's convention, you'd also know what they meant by "someone special." Stereotypes exist for a reason, and I always like to think my dad was not the stereotypical dour, grim and humorless person in the black suit and slicked hair looking to upsell that bronze casket that seemed to permeate the profession. Those were other guys' dads.

Still, Dad had certainly been at it long enough.

Born in Charlotte in 1945, my dad was the youngest of three children of E.C. and Clara Copeland. His two older sisters, Mary Jane and Eleanor, doted on their baby brother. My grandfather, an insurance salesman, was apparently a well-meaning man, but he and my grandmother went through a tough period where living situations were always itinerant. A look at my grandfather's ledger books would show that the monthly income outdid the monthly expenses, but only by a smidge. It certainly wasn't enough paper money to wad a shotgun.

They finally settled in Greer, South Carolina, when my dad was in elementary school. A small upstate town that marked the halfway point between Greenville and Spartanburg, Greer was at least considered a safe place to raise a family, though the small downtown and few restaurants and car dealerships certainly didn't seem promising to the naked eye, at least back then. By age 14, my dad had wandered down to the funeral home in his residential neighborhood to inquire about work.

What made him go there we'll never know (though I suspect his own dad had something to do with it), but the work he found there after school hours and in the summers - when he wasn't picking peaches at the Greer peach farms - came in useful four years later when his dad, E.C., died from a blood clot in his lungs. His older sisters already having left the nest, my dad was still home with a suddenly widowed mother and wondering what next step of his own to take.

At the funeral home down the street he'd mainly done the kind of chores expected of a teenage boy. Cutting the grass, washing the windows, moving the chairs in place for a service but simultaneously observing all that went on around him felt natural.

He moved to working with another funeral home in Spartanburg and helping out their ambulance service while attending Spartanburg Methodist Junior College and still living at home.

He had enough fun in Spartanburg to make him want to stay within the business. College dates often ended up on a tour of the casket display room, a kind of litmus test for the kind of girl he knew would make it past the first date. If it was their idea of "fun," or at least if they weren't scared away by it, he deemed them the kind of girl to take to The Beacon Drive-In for milkshakes.

Another time at the Spartanburg funeral home, he witnessed a coworker stick his hand inside a refrigerated Coke machine.

"What are you doing?" he asked the man.

"Just get behind that open door and watch."

Dad did as he was told and watched as a hearse pulled into the garage. Another co-worker, a short, stocky man named Fred, got out of the vehicle and opened the back door. As he maneuvered the body on the stretcher and wheeled it around to the inside of the building, Fred stopped to shut the door behind him.

To do that, he had to turn around and leave the body where it was on the stretcher.

Before he could shut the door Dad was hiding behind, the other co-worker jumped out from hiding and stuck his cold hand on Fred's neck.

Fred ended up leaving the doors and stretcher behind as he ran back into the garage, jumped on top of the hearse, put a dent in the hood and left the remains of his bladder.

The laughs were worth my dad and his co-worker having to clean up the mess.

While hijinks are always great, when it was time to get serious months later, Dad left the South altogether to live in Ohio while attending the ominously named Cincinnati College of Mortuary Science. He did well academically because it was a subject that obviously interested him, but he also learned to eat his grits with sugar on top the way they did there.

When he moved back to South Carolina after receiving his degree, he enlisted in the U.S. Army at arguably the height of the Vietnam War. He was still serving in 1967 when he came home for leave one weekend.

By that point my grandmother had made an arrangement with nearby Winthrop University to house Education majors in their last semester of student teaching. Why keep a house with three bedrooms all to herself?

My mother, at the time a Winthrop student from Beaufort named Judy Reames, was, therefore, living with her at the time when my grandmother announced that her "little boy" would be visiting for the weekend. When he came in for breakfast the next morning, his little head barely fit through the little doorway.

Needless to say, as these stories go, after an honorable discharge from the Army in 1968 he and my mom got married and, after briefly starting their married life in Spartanburg, they moved back to mom's hometown on the coast.

Then, as now, Beaufort was a closely-knit coastal community made up of retirees, military families and those in the professional class wishing to soak up sun and surf and the occasional named hurricane. Neither as big as Savannah nor as old as Charleston, Beaufort was the charming, smaller-scale envy of both.

Looking for work in Beaufort, Dad met up with a local funeral director so he could inquire about putting his mortuary science skills to use. What that funeral director, the locally legendary Johnny Morrall didn't know was that Dad was not only young but also ambitious. By 1976, Morrall-Copeland Funeral Home had become simply Copeland Funeral Home, as Dad bought the business outright and Mr. Morrall returned to his many other business ventures.

At some point Dad owned the house that later became the Rhett House Inn, an upscale bed and breakfast downtown. Of course, he used it as a funeral home. It must have been fun working downtown at that time when the City of Beaufort was growing in population if not in commerce. From the porch of the funeral home you could see glimpses of the Beaufort River if not taste some of the salt in the breeze. Humid summers were diluted only by the cover provided by the numerous oak trees overhead.

The first floor of the house, constructed in 1820, was where bodies were prepared. The second floor (just above ground level) was where offices and viewing rooms were located. The third floor was where Dad had an apprentice embalmer living, and apparently he did not live on that third floor alone.

One night when he was working alone, he heard a sound in the hall just outside his bedroom door.

"I caught a glimpse of an old man wearing a black top hat and cape," he told me. "When I turned my head to get a good look at him, he had disappeared."

Funeral homes are intimidating enough without being housed in a century-old building with ghosts. Not to mention people just weren't dying at a rate quick enough to sustain either a handsome profit or my dad's interest. He eventually sold the building and shut down the business.

My sister was born in 1974 and she and Mom and Dad were a happy threesome. By 1979, when I came along, Dad had already been elected to the Beaufort County School Board and was considering his first run for Beaufort County Coroner, but had, as mentioned, momentarily left the funeral business. He had opened up Lowcountry Realty by that point and was still finding himself looking for ways to get his creative and business juices flowing.

He'd also helped start the local ambulance service, where his greatest call while on duty was going down to the Beaufort Marina to help my uncle out of the water and into Beaufort Memorial Hospital. My uncle had been water skiing and looked ashore to wave at a pretty girl in a revealing bathing suit when he skied headfirst into a parked boat.

He was also present during the second-most circulated ambulance service story from that time, when the body of a drowned fisherman was brought to the emergency room of the hospital. As they cut open the deceased man's clothing, they discovered a couple of pounds of shrimp falling out of his boots. One emergency worker gathered the shrimp and a bag of ice and took the shrimp home to cook that evening.

Still, for Dad there were empires on the horizon that went far beyond fishing his brother-in-law out of the river or not wasting semi-fresh shrimp. I have no doubt that when I was born, back when having a male child was considered having a rightful heir, Dad probably thought I could one day inherit the family business, whether it was funeral home or real estate or growing rose bushes. It's a natural thought, especially for someone who never saw the promise of working and living alongside his own dad come to fruition.

One reason I think Dad was drawn to the field was his true desire to be helpful. In the moments between the death of a loved one, no matter how unexpected or routine, one of the first things to do is call someone to take care of the body. Dad simply wanted to be on the other end of the line when they called.

He wanted the business, yes, but he was even better with grieving people than he was with the scientific aspect of the mortuary field.

"Funerals are for the living," was one of his favorite sayings, as he knew that the service is to help someone say goodbye in a dignified manner. The deceased person is almost immaterial at that point, having moved on to some other metaphysical realm.

I suppose I should stop here and offer some sort of physical description of Curt Copeland so you'd get an idea of his stature in 1979. It's always easier to picture someone in your mind when you can piece it together with adjectives.

Only able to describe how I knew him from the time I was small, I can say that he was definitely not small. Standing fully straight, he was about 6'4 and 175 pounds. Tall and relatively skinny, as evidenced on vacation when he went crazy and sometimes wore shorts, he was most comfortable in suits that he wore for funerals, always various shades of black or navy blue. For casual wear, which included relaxing on the couch or working in the yard, he favored khaki pants and a button-down oxford. For whatever reason he hated being tied down to anything - his shoes were always slip-ons without laces and his pants were called Sansabelts, aka no need for a waist-tightening pants-holder.

His family background was largely Irish and English, which did not fully account for his darker olive skin and above-average sized nose. His hair and skin were dark enough that when he briefly grew a mustache in the early 80's, he looked like a no bueno Spanish soap opera actor. My own hair is lighter and thicker, as is my mid-section. The nose was the only thing I genetically inherited, as the promised height never came to fruition.

As a baseball player in my youth, it was assumed I'd reach my dad's height and my coaches always put me at first base. I loved first base, being able to be a part of any hit on the infield and stretching and diving while trying to keep a foot on the bag after errant throws. By high school, however, I was already looking up at other teammates and it was clear that unless a drastic growth spurt occurred I was never going to reach 6 feet. I was moved to second base and outfield, where height wasn't treasured. I withered like a dandelion cast into the wind and to this day prefer the novelty of the first baseman.

My nose, like my dad's, just kept growing. Unlike him, though, my personality didn't. He genuinely enjoyed talking to and getting to know people. He was as comfortable with a small audience of royal family members as he was with the clerks at The Pantry gas station. His voice could carry and he could systematically work a room from left to right to ensure he spoke to everyone and everyone spoke to him.

He was also unafraid of voicing an opinion, no matter the subject. Absorbing news was a pastime to him. Tom Brokaw's nightly news was only switched over to Dan Rather during commercials. Dad loved microphones and crowds and was happy in front of both. He liked to emcee festivals and events and had no issue telling complete strangers they were terrible drivers.

In fact, for years he kept a folder of correspondence with both families he'd served and people he'd ticked off. The letters in the folder were about anything from people he'd written to because they'd gotten upset with him taking so long at the post office to people he'd upset behind or in front of him in traffic. One time he even wrote the owner of a gas station to apologize, sarcastically, about asking for his money back when a pre-paid pump ran out of gas and the clerk told him to wait his turn in line.

Another piece of correspondence that he kept was with the pastor who performed the marriage ceremony for my parents in 1968. The pastor, Dr. George Jones, was also a friend and supporter of a competitor funeral home in town. Apparently hurting his business interests caused Dr. Jones to, in his own words, "hate" my dad. When Dr. Jones returned to Beaufort in 2004 for a celebration of the church's history, my dad asked Jones if he still hated him. Dr. Jones accordingly said "I probably hate you even more." It turns out he was as human as the country singer George Jones, and not quite as divine.

Next to all the nasty letters were heartfelt notes thanking him for his help during their own personal times of need. To his credit, he kept mementoes of both the good and the bad. It was in keeping with the perception of him in the community -

people loved him and hated him but rarely felt lukewarm or indifferent.

As a result of being witness to these extremes, I've always preferred the quiet solitude of the background and the distinct pleasure of being completely non-confrontational. Steady, inoffensive exchanging of pleasantries and exceptional averageness has always served me well. Mostly.

You can either end up being just like a parent, or you can subconsciously or overtly end up being the complete opposite. I chose the latter, though I'm still not sure if I was aware of my efforts. I am built - physically and temperamentally - like my grandfather, my mom's dad. His influence on me was immense, but that's a story for another book. I just knew that the limelight that my dad never shied from and sometimes sought was not something I wanted to ever be in the room with in case it actually ever caught me, too. Still, he always cast a large figurative and literal shadow that I could never quite escape.

It wasn't that he didn't try - he absolutely did. He escaped to an outdoor carpentry and woodworking shop as often as he could and often invited me to join him, but I'm no Bob Vila.

He liked music and recognized that I did, too, so he bought me my first electric guitar, though his own music preference was more of the piano and light saxophone variety. He couldn't sit still long enough to read books, as I did, and he certainly wasn't into sports with as much enthusiasm as I had. I remember trying to tell him about the greatness of Roger Clemens one time when a baseball game was on our TV.

"Dad, if Clemens strikes out this batter he's going to win his 18th game this year and should be a lock for another Cy Young Award!" I told him.

"Oh really?" he said from the couch.

"Yeah, I bet he can probably even lower his ERA to under 2.90…"

I never finished the sentence because I looked over at him and he was snoring. Not even a sarcastic snore, but a "you've just literally bored me to sleep" kind of snore. There was just little for us to bond over and by the time I was 30 - time to talk to a father as more of a peer - he was gone.

For years a family joke was that no one even knew about me. My sister, five and a half years older than I am and long my dad's pride and joy, was someone he always talked about. They were close in temperament and she was the proto-typical "daddy's girl." All through my life, it seemed, I would meet people in the community and the same exchange would happen.

"Hi, I'm Ryan Copeland."

"Copeland? You related to the funeral home people?" they'd say.

"Yeah, that's my dad."

"Oh!" they would reply, genuinely surprised. "I never knew Curt had a son! I knew about his daughter…"

I can't count how many times I had that actual conversation with someone. It's almost as if I were hidden in a closet for most of my life and allowed out only for food and the occasional shower.

The thing is, it just never failed to amuse me. You never quite learn how to reply to that kind of information - people not knowing you existed. It doesn't bother me; I just found it humorous. So no, my dad and I were not complete opposites, but we kind of existed in circles around each other. If we were parts of a Venn diagram, we'd have a very small overlapped middle.

One of the greatest moments of my life was witnessing the time my dad got mad at my sister. He'd always been quick to correct me and I think he was just different in disciplining me than he was with Shelley. Boys need more order to keep from getting out of control, I guess, but I also need more motivation.

He knew I was dumb, in other words.

Still, I wasn't the one who drove his car into the ditch when practicing getting it into the driveway. He hated carelessness and that was the one instance my sister displayed it.

I watched from the comfort of my living room as my sister, standing in the yard, tearfully explained what happened. My dad, having none of that business, yelled at her using exaggerated hand motions. I'd seen that show a hundred times before but usually right in front of my own face.

As he gesticulated wildly a screwdriver he was holding flew loose from his hand. It went careening across the yard and past my sister. From my sideways vantage point it looked like he'd thrown it at her. That's the story I've stuck to because it gives me the most pleasure.

In fact I'm sure I was smiling.

At least I was until my mom walked in and told me to go back into my bedroom because I didn't need to see what I was seeing.

"But it's just getting good!" I whined.

I know she had a smile, too.

Like I said, though, even if his bond with my sister was so natural that he got mad at her exactly once during my childhood, he did try to bond with me, especially if it meant going out of town to do so.

For someone as busy as he was, I never appreciated the simple sacrifice of leaving town. On every trip we ever took, as soon as we hit the county line on the way out he would radio the emergency services people.

"Dispatch, 601," he'd say.

"601, go ahead," would come the reply.

"I'll be (make up a number here that represents the correct call number because I don't remember) until 1800 hours on Tuesday," he would say, letting them know he was gone and they should go down the public service food chain if any unnatural death occurred.

Some trips, like one to the Savannah Civic Center to watch NWA Wrestling, weren't overnight. Dad hated professional wrestling but realized I was stupid and enjoyed it, so he took me and my friend Noah Denton to a "house show," a non-televised event during the heyday of The Nature Boy Ric Flair.

During a tag team match between The Rock and Roll Express and their rivals The Midnight Express, the

Midnights' manager, Jim Cornette, got caught in the ropes and hit repeatedly by Robert Gibson of The R&R. I looked over and definitely caught my dad laughing so hard he was choking, so thank you, Jim Cornette, for making that evening palatable for my dad.

I halfway expected, based on his momentary laughter, for us to return to Beaufort and make Saturday Night World Championship Wrestling on TBS a regular viewing for both of us, but that never materialized.

Another trip that did take us out of town was to see a Braves game in Atlanta. We'd been going as a family to Braves games since the team was awful, and the empty stands allowed plenty of space for children like me to stand in line to be terrified by Chief-Noc-a-Homa, a Braves mascot who was somehow less happy to be in the stadium than fans and most of the team.

Anyway, Dad decided we'd go to a random game one weekend in the middle of the Braves great run of division championships in the 90's, and it would just be him, my friend Taylor Ingram and me. Again, he knew better than to take me to something alone because it would be a quiet, awkward ride.

When Taylor and I got into the back seat of Dad's Ford Crown Victoria, we found it already occupied by two urns.

"Ah...don't worry about those, I just need to drop them off on the way."

So the five of us started off down the road towards Atlanta, but somewhere in the fields of rural Georgia - I want to say we were close to Metter - the Crown Vic (as I've just started calling it) started to have engine trouble.

My dad immediately got on his big ass bag phone, as you do when you've got car trouble, and called his local Ford mechanic back in Beaufort. It was the early days of cell phone usage and that bag phone was rudimentary - couldn't take pictures or anything - but it connected Dad to someone at the dealership. Together they determined he needed to get it looked at ASAP.

Sensing it might be awhile, both Taylor and I fell asleep in the back seat. When we woke up, unfortunately, we saw nothing but vegetable fields on both sides of us (corn? wheat?) and a man with a beard and long blond hair driving the car.

I looked at Taylor and he looked at me and we both kinda shrugged our shoulders and went along for the murder ride.

After a few minutes, the man made it back to a double-garage mechanic shop that appeared out of nowhere in the middle of the corn/wheat fields.

Dad was standing outside drinking a Coke and casually talking to another man who was nearly identical to the serial killer/mechanic driving the car, only slightly larger and with darker hair.

I'm fairly certain that leaving two kids in the back of your car while a stranger says "lemme take her for a spin and hear how she sounds" is a rule in the book of "Things We Don't Do," but Dad was always looking for ways to toughen me up.

I didn't ask him where we were or why he'd left us both (well, the four of us including the urns) in the backseat, but the two mechanics did some things under the hood and told us we were good to go.

Dad paid them and we said goodbye to Lynyrd and his brother Skynyrd and were on our way, but when we finally arrived in Atlanta to see the Braves play, all we encountered was a rain storm over Fulton County Stadium.

We got to the parking lot and I opened my door a little too aggressively, hitting the car next to us. My dad pulled out sixty dollars and paid the guy and said "sorry, my son is not the brightest." I got a ten minute lecture about carelessness from the parking lot to the stadium while Taylor looked like he wished we'd left him in a corn/wheat field.

The rain continued, though we did see a crazy man walking past us near the vendors saying he was going to "kill Bobby Cox," over and over. What the Braves coach had to do with the weather I'm not sure, but it was fun to watch from a distance.

After the game was officially canceled we slept at our hotel near the interstate, got up the next day and stopped at a Krispy Kreme for breakfast. Instead of doughnuts, Taylor and I focused on getting some gum out of the giant bubble gum machine, but all it did was eat our quarters.

Dad went up to the counter and said "hey, the gumball machine ate my kid's quarters, is there anyone who can get it open?"

"What'd ya want me to do about it, pal, I got customers here?!" said the man at the register.

I knew what was coming.

Dad reached into his wallet and pulled out a $20 bill and threw it on the counter.

"Get your damn machine fixed," he said.

He pulled me and Taylor with him as he walked back by us. We left without gum or doughnuts but with a certain amount of pride for sticking it to The Man and his worthless gumball racket.

It was a trip from hell for Dad, and he probably thought it was par for the course. I know without a doubt he'd have rather been home working - minding the store - than making bad memories. I mean, people who died while he was gone weren't going to bury themselves.

I don't blame him now or then. He tried, mostly in vain. The effort was sometimes exhausting and for someone who slept as little as he did, already more than he could afford.

Hopefully you now have a better physical, if not temperamental description of him, but I can also think of no better illustration for our innate differences than one particular morning's drive to school. Dad generally went into work much later than my mom, whose work as a high school teacher had her there in the dark every morning. As his own boss, Dad could afford to drive us to school and drop us off in the school drop-off circle every morning before going back home and getting showered and dressed for the day.

One morning on the way to Lady's Island Middle School, I was excited to put my new cassette tape into his car and listen to my music on the way from our home in Mossy Oaks all the way across the bridge to school. The music was old but the tape was new - Timepieces: The Best of Eric Clapton. I'd discovered classic rock by then and was as much in love with the song "Layla" as Clapton was with Pattie Boyd when he wrote that particular song about her.

From the opening riff I could tell that my dad didn't like the song. I was rocking out inside my head as neither of us said a word - again, not necessarily anything unusual as I didn't like talking in the morning. But at some point after we'd crossed the bridge, the song slowed from the hard, painful rocker of the first three minutes into Duane Allman's mournful slide guitar and the piano and strings that closed out the final four minutes of the song. It was at that point - rocking over, sentimental love song beginning - that I ejected the tape.

"Why'd you do that?" my dad asked as we pulled into school. "It was just starting to get good."

CHAPTER III.

TOP 10 THINGS YOU SHOULD KNOW BEFORE YOU GO:

These are mostly little etiquette rules that I learned growing up in the business:

1. Don't walk on top of graves in the cemetery. It's considered rude and disrespectful to just walk on a grave. They make horror movies with plots based on the dangers of doing just this. Of course, if you're going to mourn or place flowers or whatever, you have to make it accessible, but you should always try to walk sideways towards the gravestone, not across rows and rows of graves. Once you reach the row where your particular gravestone is, walk through the presumed "foot" of the grave, never the head. Once you've had this pointed out to you once, believe me, it's not something you'll forget about. You should also not wave and shout a friendly "hello!" to anyone else in the cemetery. It's not the time or place.

2. Church trucks - aka the wheeled bases that carry caskets - are fantastic for children getting a running

start and jumping onto while rolling down a long, empty hall. They'll go a good fifteen feet after you jump on and they're nearly impossible to steer, so I suggest having drywall that is easily patched nearby. As soon as the door opens and a family walks in to discuss funeral plans, however, it's best to hop back off and wait for them to leave. They're a fantastic alternative to a skateboard, though there's not currently a Nintendo game featuring Tony Hawk, so know that going into the sport.

3. The smell of embalming fluid, once it enters an olfactory nerve, is difficult to get out. It's also hard to describe - the amalgam of chemicals is distinct. While you would think it would be limited to the embalming room, you'd be wrong. Once a bottle of it spills in the back seat of a van there is not enough Lysol in the world to erase it. This is not asking for a friend. This is speaking from experience.

4. A funeral chapel, the little sanctuary area of a funeral home, is a great place to test the sound system when you're alone and you're 10. There's usually a little control room in the back of a chapel that houses all the lights, sound and video equipment for the chapel. Flashing the lights on and off enough times to induce

a seizure is only fun when no one else is watching you. Well, it could be fun if you do it while someone's in there and you come out screaming "did y'all feel that too?!" The tape player connected to the sound system? It's usually for the organ hymns that play in the background during a service. It's almost never for "The Monkees Greatest Hits," which does not need to blast when a grieving family is just down the hall. At that point it's less about "The Last Train to Clarksville" and more about "the last time your dad takes you to his work and leaves you alone."

5. No, none of us in the family funeral business live at the morgue. Yes, some funeral homes are still housed within a family's living quarters, as depicted in the movie *My Girl* and the television show *Six Feet Under*. Those families had more going wrong for them than just living in a funeral parlor, however. And for what those depictions got wrong, my dad could and would have written his own book. Although he mostly enjoyed watching reruns of *Quincy, M.E.*, I can't even get started on how he felt about WWE wrestling superstar The Undertaker. But no, most funeral homes in modern times are separate places of business.

6. Even when you don't live at the funeral home, you all spend enough time there to qualify. It's why there's a room with a cot and a shower, for those nights when you're there while a body runs its course through the crematory. A funeral home is even a great place to have a birthday party, apparently. My sister had her 30th birthday party there because it fell on a Friday, the 13th and also funeral homes are known to be party spots. They set up ladders to walk under, there were stuffed black cats everywhere. It was...unique. As close as she and my dad were, it was also not unexpected. For the record, I did not eat the cake.

7. We've heard every joke before and none of them are funny. "What's your slogan, 'you stab 'em we slab 'em?'" Not funny, even in 1967 when it first appeared. "People are always dying to get in your business?" That one required even less effort to come up with. "Why are you here, no one's dead!" Can't count how many times that one offended my dad, not because he was easily offended (he was, though) but because it was unoriginal. Everyone who's ever been friends with a funeral director has heard it, and none of them have ever been amused.

8. Yes, just as much as the bad jokes bother them, the humanity in good funeral directors comes out in other ways as well. They do not become immune to death, despite dealing in it every day. Dad had many sleepless nights when there was the body of a young child alone at the funeral home waiting for a service. Tiny caskets - which were always free of charge because no one even liked having to make them - were bothersome. Even worse was the angst I could see on my dad's face when he had to tell a coworker that her husband had died mid-jog of an undetected heart issue. He showed up to her house and she thought it was a work-related matter, which it was, but also much worse. He was trained for her reaction, of course, but being there in triplicate roles - Coroner, funeral director and friend - takes its toll on anyone. That was not an easy day, week or month for him.

9. Moving over or slowing down for funeral traffic isn't just respectful, it's safe. You never know when processions heading from a church to a cemetery are going to go through a red light. You also shouldn't break in on the line or honk at the procession, unless you know the person in the back of the hearse and

you have their express, written consent to "honk at me when I'm dead!"

10. Like a country doctor bartering fresh farm eggs for delivering a baby in the middle of the night in rural Nebraska, funeral directors will also accept other items "in lieu of payment." It's how I got a model train set when I was young. A man from New Jersey had passed away and his widow, instead of paying for funeral costs, agreed to exchange her late husband's model train set (which took up the better part of any normal sized room) in the trust that I'd have more fun with it than would she. I wasn't really into trains at the time but quickly learned the difference between a coupler and a cradle. The value was at least greater than the 1988 Chevy Silverado I'd get a couple of years later when Dad accepted it from a widow in a similar situation. I don't think he technically died in the truck, though there was a bullet hole in the glass that had to be fixed and the widow certainly didn't need it sitting in the yard. So I literally drove a dead man's truck for a while in high school. I loved everything but the brakes, which were "loose" at best and required much forethought when a stop sign was coming up in the road. It was a tan color and I called it the "Brown

Angel of Death," but it was fun for a couple years. I mean, I guess there were technically worse things for him to bring home from work.

TOP FIVE PEOPLE YOU DIDN'T KNOW DABBLED IN THE FUNERAL INDUSTRY:

1. Angelina Jolie - the one who first married Billy Bob and then took a step down to marry Brad Pitt. Her roles in film, like her personality on the red carpet, tend towards the dark side. She apparently got a mail-order funeral directors license, not unlike the people you read about who store hundreds of bodies in the freezers of their funeral homes before they're caught. The funeral business wasn't for her, after all, to the great delight of anyone who's a fan of *Gone in 60 Seconds*. Both of you.

2. Marshall White - never heard of him either? Don't tell him to his face if you ever meet him. The former World's Strongest Man competitor could throw you into a casket, throw that casket into an 18-wheeler, then haul the 18-wheeler to a junkyard with nothing

more than a harness and a Gatorade. If you've never been afraid of a mortician, now's your chance.

3. Harold Ford, Sr. - Harold Ford, Jr's father. Who's Harold Ford, Jr? Harold Ford, Sr's son, of course. But no, really, they are both prominent politicians from Tennessee. Ford, Jr. was once on a short list of prospects, but Ford, Sr., also a former US Congressman, had Ford and Sons Funeral Home as a nice little "fallback."

4. Elizabeth Meyer - technically, the former funeral director for the Frank E. Campbell Funeral Chapel in New York City does more than dabble. She's on the list less for who she is than for what she's done for Campbell: the funeral home of choice for John Lennon, Jackie Kennedy Onassis, Jim Henson, Biggie Smalls and Walter Cronkite. In her time at the funeral chapel, she helped arrange a tour bus for the funeral of guitar legend Les Paul, a Ferrari next to the casket of a millionaire car collector, and was asked to check for the brain of the deceased Sunny von Bulow by von Bulow's son. The brain was missing, but we only know all this because Meyer wrote about her experiences!

5. Danny DeVito - the dad from *Matilda*? No, no, the Penguin from *Batman Returns*. Wait, no, Schwarzenegger's twin in *Twins*. Yes, it's true, the boss from *Taxi* was taught how to style hair from his sister, a hair salon owner in Manhattan. A lot of her clientele was the recently deceased, so she'd send her brother Danny, aka Frank Reynolds on *It's Always Sunny in Philadelphia* to style the hair of women who wouldn't talk back or move around much.

THE STEPS OF A FUNERAL

1. Obviously, the first step occurs when someone dies. I'm saying "someone" and not "you" because presumably you're reading this while still alive. But when someone you know or love passes away whether by accident on the job, naturally at home, unfortunately in the hospital or tragically not by their own hands, someone has to do something with the body. That's where a funeral home comes in. If that person did not have pre-arrangements made with a funeral home then their next of kin will have to make the decision which funeral home to use. At that point

someone makes the call to the funeral home and workers from there - sometimes the funeral director/owner themselves but more often not - will come and take the body from the hospital or home. The body will generally be taken away in whatever shape it's in and be "prepared" and cleaned up at the funeral home. Believe me when I say I've seen a murder victim under a sheet at the funeral home before preparation. Those are images everyone involved wants to erase as quickly as possible, including the embalmer.

2. The second step is preparation of the body itself. Per your wishes your loved one will be embalmed, i.e. washed down with disinfectant and cleared of veinal blood. The blood is then replaced arterially with a chemical agent - usually formaldehyde - that helps "preserve" some kind of liquidity to the skin. We won't talk about cavity embalming, but know that it's a thing. Unless your loved one is Jewish and will be buried before sundown the next day, then you have no need for any type of embalming. That's the entire point - the funeral home should honor both law and the decision of the departed. It's kind of gross, but Vladimir Lenin's body is embalmed every few months, despite the fact

that he's been dead since 1924. On the other hand, it was claimed that Pope John Paul, II did not go through the embalming process despite being on display on a catafalque in Vatican City for a week. More recently, former Auburn football coach Pat Dye was simply wrapped in a sheet at his death and placed directly in a grave at the foot of a tree on his farm, a simple and eco-friendly ceremony that is growing in popularity.

3. While the body of your loved one is being prepared, you will be asked to come in and meet with the funeral director to decide how to best memorialize the deceased. This includes bringing burial clothes and selecting a casket, if necessary. Of course, choosing cremation takes away the need for both of those so deciding on a tasteful urn may be your only concern. For services, you may decide that there should be a "wake" or more commonly what we call a "visitation" in the South. This is more of a "drop-in" usually held at the funeral home the night before the service. This is part of a long tradition of "staying up with the dead." I'm only two generations removed from this practice myself, as I remember hearing my grandmother talk about when she was a child and her uncle, a not-so-

nice man they called Uncle Willie, died. The day after he died his body was placed in a casket that stayed at my grandmother's childhood home until his funeral the next day. The adults took turns wearily sitting in the living room with the body all through the night, but the kids, most notably my grandmother's brother, had more fun. His idea was to push his siblings into the room with the casket, shut the door behind them and scream "Get her Willie, get her!" Anyway, the more modern visitation just involved giving people a two-hour window to come to the funeral home, stand in line to hug the grieving family, sign a guest book, take a look at the body in the open casket and say "looks better than he did all last decade!" and move back out into the night.

4. In addition to the visitation decisions, you will be asked to help plan out a funeral service. If you belong to a church, it's customary to hold the service there. This means the funeral director will call in the pastor of the church to make sure there are accommodations that can be made. Once the date and time and venue of the service is arranged, it's time to decide what hymns (if any) should be played. What verses of the Bible or terrible Emily Dickinson poetry books should

be read? Who should sing or play guitar in an awkward folk melody? Who will give the eulogy? Are there even people around who can say nice things with a PG rating? Which six members of my friends or family circle can be counted on to serve as pallbearers and not drop the casket? These are the things you have to consider.

5. Once you've added the costs of all of the above, you'll have to haggle with your insurance company on paying funeral costs. You'll be in no mood for dealing with that, so a good funeral director could and should help negotiate and communicate on your behalf. Yes, everything a funeral home does costs money, but you should never feel as if they're trying to take advantage of you during a vulnerable moment.

6. You might have to pick out some pictures from a family photo album or digital collection for playing in a loop on a television the night of the visitation. Think of it as those "in remembrance" sections at the Oscars ceremony, only no one will clap because your loved one isn't that famous.

7. The final steps-the ones that come after you've already supplied the info for the obituary, chosen the casket, the pallbearers, the speakers, the clothes, the

registry book, the venue, etc.-are choosing the gravesite and place for a post-burial reception. Temporary grave markers are almost always placed at the site of the grave, even when you can tell that it's "freshly dug." That keeps you from having to feel stressed about getting a permanent marker ordered from a monument company. As for the place for the reception, or what I call the "after party," it's usually right after the funeral and committal service in the church social hall. I've also seen it take place at a home, on the bluff downtown, even in a caravan headed to the beach. The point is, people will want to stand around and converse, not to mention eat some cold fried chicken that someone's great-aunt lovingly cooked early that same morning. Accept it graciously.

CHAPTER IV.

Learning to drive is something to which most teens in the 20th Century looked forward. When I got my permit, my sudden mobility just made it easier for me to help out at the funeral home. I could now get there on my own - in my sister's hand-me-down 1989 Ford Mustang - and work at my own pace. Oddly enough, when I got out there, I started in the "family business" much the same way my dad had when he was my age.

I spent most of my time on a tractor.

No, I don't mean a riding lawnmower, I mean a tractor that had steps to climb onto it. Beaufort Memorial Gardens, the cemetery Dad owned that was adjacent to the funeral home, was and is only about half full. Or half empty, depending on your view. When he bought it from Leroy Keyserling in the early 1980's, it was even less (or more!) so. All that meant was that half the acreage - in full sun with no hint of shade - needed constant mowing because the grass was not interrupted by pesky gravesites.

Keep in mind that I also started working at Sears during the summers beginning when I was 15.

"You don't have to work for me," my dad said. "But you do have to work for someone."

Of course that meant working at Sears unloading trucks and putting out stock items and loading customer purchases, but also working at the funeral home whenever necessary. For a lot less pay.

So it was that I began on weekends and other "days off" from Sears cutting the grass in the large, unfilled fields of the cemetery. Sitting on top of the old diesel tractor gave me plenty of time to think, surrounded by graves and dense, wooded forestry. I probably could have spent time pondering my existential crisis of being stuck, literally, between two worlds. As it was, it was way more fun to hit the switch that operated the blades and gun the manual transmission in 6th gear and think about good nicknames for myself. "Hayseed" came to mind, but I'd probably have to buy a good straw hat for that one. "Dr. Death" seemed to require a degree I didn't have.

Either way, the job I did was so good that I ended up graduating from the large tractor with the pull-behind blade attachment to a smaller, zero-turn radius mower that could get in between the flat headstones. That went well for about half an hour, total, before I got too close and clipped one of those permanent, metal vases that holds the artificial flowers. I stopped to look at what I'd done and saw that there was no way to fix it quickly.

I decided I'd need to tell my dad that I did it, but I wanted to finish cutting around the rest of the flat headstones first. I hadn't been back at it too long before I clipped another one. This one completely broke off from its base and the blades ate up the flowers that went with it.

When I was done I went inside to confess.

"You've cost me at least $80!" he said.

I decided I didn't even want to tell him about the garden hose I also hit with the blade and busted. I'd try to blame that one on "an animal."

"Son," he said, "you've got to be more careful. You can't get cutesy."

That was his word for when I'd gone too far making jokes or being flippant or just not paying attention to what I was doing. Cutesy. When things go to shit it's because you weren't paying enough attention and got too cutesy. The first time I used it as an adult I slapped my own cheek.

So I was taken back off the grass-cutting duties for a while, at least around headstones. The tractor mowing continued in the fields, where I could only maybe lose control and hit a tree while daydreaming about earning the nickname "Porkchop" or something similar. Still, it was one step above being handed a shovel and being told to dig until you hit water.

Speaking of shovels, ironically the next summer that was what I was given, but it was to dig 30 holes in which to plant some upright ligustrum. Why would a funeral home need 30 ligustrum? To cover the garage and crematory from the view of the general public, of course. That job took me two days to get finished, but to see the results of my labor now, you wouldn't even know what goes on behind the foliage.

Not long after I had dutifully planted the shrubs, I got a call from my dad's assistant asking if I could take a couple of people to Savannah. I had proven my worth, I guess, in the experience I had driving my truck over to nearby metropolitan Yemassee getting plants at a nursery there. I returned not only with all the plants intact but I didn't hit one gravestone or pedestrian on the trip!

So I accepted the Savannah job and arrived expecting to have to take a nice couple from Columbus to the airport or something. I even cleaned out the cab of my truck. All the assistant said was "a couple of people."

Again, I was dumb.

Leaving my truck in the funeral home driveway upon arrival the next day, I was instructed instead to take the company van to Savannah. I'd have two "drop-offs" to make - one was to the airport, incidentally. The other was to another funeral home on Stephenson Avenue.

If you're wondering about my cargo, you're right. Two deceased people - lined up in heavy duty boxes next to each other - were in the back of the van. The passenger seat was the only other seat in the vehicle besides my own and yes, it was the same van where formaldehyde had stained and permanently odored the carpet.

I was 16 and soon headed onto I-95 to get to the Savannah Airport. My passengers were quiet and so was the ride. In addition to the smell, the van featured a radio that didn't work. It was just as well because getting off onto the right exit required me to pay attention to the right signage. Throw in the fact that I needed to drive around and find the cargo loading area of the airport and my relative youth and inexperience with driving in "big city traffic" in general and I was lucky to be able to concentrate.

I was also lucky that this was a pre-9/11 airport.

The security guards at the cargo gate didn't even check what I had in the back. The "Copeland Funeral Home" license plate on the front of the van might have given it away, but they still could have made sure it wasn't a giant box of weed or cocaine or assault rifles.

They just directed me to the back of the airport and I drove up towards a Delta holding dock. Two guys in those overall bibs with the Delta logo stepped out from under the plane and waved me over. I got out and opened up the back and helped the guys get a long, white box with a FedEx label out and onto a cart. They did the rest as I said goodbye to whomever was in there. I didn't even catch his name.

Now it was time to make my way from the airport to Abercorn in Savannah. I needed to take another box there for cremation. Dad had the crematory built in Beaufort the year before but something in the heating element of the retort needed repair, so I had to drive all their cremation business to a friendly funeral home just over the border in neighboring Georgia.

When I arrived, I pulled under the carport on the side entrance for what I assumed was "easy removal," but I was told by a gentleman in a dark suit (what else?) to drive over to the brick building about 50 yards away.

There, the view obstructed by absolutely nothing, was a brick furnace with three slots in the middle, for lack of a better word. I mean, it was obvious that it wasn't pizza being fired up in that kiln. Those middle slots had doors on them, so the woman in the back of my van was unloaded and put onto a slab to go into the slot. I watched her go in with the door shut behind her. The men doing it were gentle, taking their time and handling it as delicately as they would a porcelain doll from the Ming Dynasty.

It was all very dignified and horrifying at the same time.

I went back inside to the funeral home office to wait it out, not even turning around to see the smoke coming out of the chimney. The inside of the office was like every funeral home office I'd ever been in - and that was more already than most "ordinary" people had. Coffee grounds that had brewed several hours earlier but were still sitting on a warming plate permeated the paperwork-filled office.

"You can just sit here for a few minutes, honey" said the woman behind the front desk. "It won't be too long."

She said it as if I'd just come into Zippy Lube and was waiting on an oil change. Still, it gave me time to observe things. Like most funeral homes, this one had a curious mix of generic beach watercolors and oil paintings of Jesus hanging on the walls. Those are the two things people coming in to make funeral arrangements want to think about - their Lord and Savior and that Great Coral Reef in the Sky.

I was also, as a teenager, the youngest person in the building by a good half-century.

I watched the traffic on Abercorn out the window for a while and listened to the one-sided phone conversations I could hear the office manager having. Before I knew it, a different man in a blue suit came and asked me if I was from Copeland's.

"Yes sir," I said.

His entire body filled the door frame, it seemed, though his head was slightly stooped forward and made his glasses slip down his nose at an awkward angle.

"Are you related to Curt or you just work for him?" he asked.

"I'm his son," I answered.

"Oh!" he laughed. "I didn't know Curt had a son!"

"I can imagine," I said.

"Well here, she's ready, and please tell Curt that Charlie gives his best," he said, handing me a small, warm tupperware box with a label on top. Even I knew it wasn't a congealed salad inside.

I took the ashes of the late Mrs. What's Her Name in my hand and got back into the van heading north. Neglecting to ask for directions home, I started out in the general direction of the bridge. I took a left out on Abercorn and then another left on Victory and before I knew it I'd somehow gotten near all the chemical plants that you could smell for miles. I could see the bridge in the distance getting farther away as I drove, presumably, towards Atlanta.

Somehow I managed to turn around and follow the Talmadge Bridge by eyesight as it got closer and make it back to Beaufort by dark. I had no complaints from my passenger, either, but it was eventually decided that I would only drive locally from that point.

Specifically, I was asked to drive the limousine at an upcoming funeral.

This was my big break! I was ready to be seen by the living in the funeral business and informally acknowledged as having shared the same last name. It was less of "this is my son with whom I am well pleased" and more of "we ran out of employees to pay and so my dumb teen son is doing this for free to give him some experience because the least he can do is drive."

If you're (luckily?) unfamiliar, the limousine is what arrives at a family's house before the funeral to transport them to the church or chapel, then takes them from there after the service to the cemetery if it's not a church graveyard within walking distance.

The family I had to pick up lived in a relatively rural neighborhood in Burton. I was already self-conscious about driving a limo because it just wasn't my style. It was even worse in an area where limos stuck out like Canadian geese in Morocco.

The day was already super-humid, so I didn't notice the sweat dripping off the forehead of the poor widow at 10:00 in the morning. She had on a dress that resembled a nightgown, though I wasn't really up on the latest women's fashion. Maybe that was a thing now. Her children soon joined her in the yard before they got in the car. An adult daughter in a skirt and what appeared to be a teenager not much younger than me with an awkwardly tied necktie came slowly towards the limo. I got out and opened the door for them like any good English butler would. I'd seen movies. I knew what was expected.

Their husband and father had passed suddenly after a massive heart attack on a local tennis court. I knew grief had many facets and could manifest itself in various ways, but it was apparent that when this man died he took all the family sanity with him.

As soon as we turned out of the driveway and headed towards the Methodist Church, it began to show.

"This thing is too tight," said the son.

"You're too fat, it's not even tied right," said the daughter.

"Yeah you better watch it with that or you'll end up like your dad," said the mom.

They were ganging up on the poor fat kid with the bad tie on the day of his own dad's funeral. This was a new family dynamic to me.

"At least I get his bike," said the boy.

"Hell no you don't!" replied his mom. "That's my way to get around now, you know my license expired."

What I'd thought at first was reference to a Harley-Davidson or maybe a Kawasaki was clearly meant to be more of a Schwinn variety of bike. Worse, there was no window to roll up between the front and back seats. I began to speed as much as I could in the long, sluggish Ford.

"I think Dad would want me to have it," said the son.

"I don't think Dad wanted you to have diabetes," replied the daughter.

This was going to be a long day.

"We'll get through this," said the mom, turning suddenly reflective and supportive. "As long as the funeral doesn't last too long outside and we can get back home. I'm already hungry."

With that I wheeled in front of the church and parked on the street, nearly hitting the curb in my rush to get the car parked and the family out of my earshot.

My duties weren't done, though, as anyone who's ever worked multiple funeral industry jobs can tell you. When I entered the church and found my dad, he was busy making sure the flowers were placed appropriately in the sanctuary. It was dark inside the stained-glass windowed church, making it even more surreal contrasted with the heat of the rising sun outside.

"Dad, these people are nuts!" I told him in a whisper.

"Some people don't know how to handle loss, that's all," he said. "They'll be fine."

I wondered how much time he'd actually spent with them.

Before I could escape, though, he told me to go back outside and stand with the three of them to make sure they waited until precisely 11:00 - Dad was a stickler for starting on time - to follow in a procession down the aisle behind the casket.

"You mean I've got to stand in the blazing sun another ten minutes for this?" said the wife when I told her they couldn't go in yet. "I don't know if I've got enough deodorant on for this!" she said, looking at her two children for approval.

I was to lead them to their seats and then walk back out of the sanctuary until I heard the final hymn playing, at which point I'd come back in and lead them back out to the waiting limo.

Being in the back of the church was always strange during a funeral. You weren't inside the sanctuary, so you could talk in a tone slightly louder than a whisper, but you weren't quite out of the building, either. You were stuck in that purgatory position between the organ music and quiet sniffling to your right and the rush of cars and blaring horns to your left, with only a set of doors on each side.

Sitting there with two other funeral home workers was like highway department pavers waiting for the roads to clear. There's not much to do but lean against the shovels and hope you don't get hit.

"You know, you remind me of your granddad," said Larry, Dad's main embalmer.

"Are you saying I'm old and overweight?" I asked.

"No," he smiled. "I mean your demeanor. It just puts me in mind of Cecil. That's a compliment."

In truth I always did take it as a compliment when someone said that. It had been years since my mom's dad died, and he was and still is my ideal for what a man should be.

"You know, that's a good point, the slugger here is kinda built like Cecil," said Asa.

Asa and Larry didn't agree on much, but here I was a unifying force in their limited conversations. Both had been working with my dad a long time, but Asa was a tough-guy

EMT, deputy coroner and embalmer. He wore lots of jewelry, including rings on almost every finger, and had a demeanor that let you know he didn't take shit from anyone. He'd been calling me "Slugger" ever since I was in 7th grade and got suspended from school for fighting in the gym.

Yes, I got in a fight in front of two P.E. classes in the gym and essentially got my ass kicked while only landing a couple of good Nolan Ryan-style noogies to my opponent's head. After the fight was broken up, I had to go to the assistant principal's office and call my dad to tell him I was being suspended. You'd think that a phone call from a child in the middle of the day would sound some kind of internal alarm, but Dad put me on hold to answer another business call.

"Sorry," I whispered to the assistant principal while covering the mouthpiece with my hand. "He'll just be a minute, he had a...very important call to take."

I stood and listened to Muzak and thanked the God of School Suspensions that my dad wasn't grasping the seriousness of the situation.

Anyway, I think Asa thought it was funny that a future librarian would try to fight in the school gym and called me Slugger relentlessly and mostly sarcastically.

Asa's colleague Larry was a little less intimidating, buttons always buttoned and ties always straight and jackets always stiffly taut over the shoulders, but he could be just as snippy when he wanted to be. He was licensed as a funeral director as well and Dad relied on him to turn a dead body into something people could look at without choking. Precision and attention to detail were Larry's game, and if a hair was out of place or the pancake makeup ran out, he could get upset easily.

Had I stayed with it, I could have learned a lot about the funeral business from both Asa and Larry.

As it was, I'd be content to wait with them while a service was going on and hope the conversation stayed to a minimum.

This day, however, there wasn't much time for anymore conversations or comparisons to grandparents because we soon had the whoosh of the double doors startling us back to reality. An usher from the church came out escorting an older gentleman by the arm and said it had gotten too hot inside the sanctuary for the man.

I'd seen *The Exorcist*. I knew this was a clear sign that the man was either the devil or one of his minions. If you get too hot inside a sanctuary it's obvious the physical reaction to Christ's presence means you are about to vomit some pea soup-looking substance. Before I could suggest checking the man's head for three sixes, Asa stood up and said the man had gotten too hot from the outdoor weather seeping in a sanctuary with an old, unreliable cooling system. The EMT in Asa took over and he told the man to lie down on the floor of the vestibule and hold his knees to his chest.

The man loosened his tie at the neck and refused to lie down. As he was heading towards the stairs to maybe sit for a minute, he collapsed. Asa reached for his cell phone and called for an ambulance, then stood over the man and shook his own head.

"Told the asshole to lie down," he said.

I was going to make a joke about just letting nature take its course and going ahead and doing a two-for-one service while we were all here, but then my dad came through the doors and said it was almost time to lead the family and the casket back out because they were on the last hymn. Seeing the situation we had in the vestibule, he went back in and motioned with his hand for the minister to tell the organist to keep playing.

While the ambulance arrived and took away the man who had collapsed and now revived, the organist played the 27th verse of Amazing Grace, which might have been a record for a Methodist church service, though certainly the Baptists had gotten carried away during a revival and sung that many before.

I finally got back down the aisle to lead the family back out and into the limo for the drive out to a small family cemetery in Grays Hill. The first few minutes of the ride were mercifully quiet, but once the cemetery came into view the conversation in the backseat struck up again.

"I don't know why your father thought he was Andre Agassi," said the widow.

"He shouldn't have been playing tennis on a public court anyway," said the son. "He was too old."

So now they'd moved on to blaming the victim for getting exercise.

"Look, Dad died doing what he loved in those long Adidas socks he loved to be in," said the daughter in defense of the recently deceased.

Saying someone died doing what they loved is only a coping mechanism for the survivors to think that right up until their loved one's heart stopped, they were genuinely enjoying life. If the dead could speak, however, their cause of death might eventually change their mind about what they considered a favorite activity.

I pulled up near a lonely tent in the middle of the cemetery. Dad had beaten me there, of course, as had the hearse. There was a water cooler set up near the tent as all the trees surrounding the cemetery were on the exterior of the gravesite. Of course this family had a plot right in the middle of the grass with no cover from the sun.

As I happily let the family out of the limo, I noticed the mom took an extra minute to put her shoes back on. Even that seemed to be something she did begrudgingly. While others from the service pulled up and got out of their cars to surround the family at the grave, I went towards the back of the crowd to observe from a distance. I thought about how strange the conversation in the limo had been and wondered where the man who'd passed out was now. My reverie of the surreal was brought back into reality when I heard the first chords of a folk song.

I turned to find a man and woman had taken center stage in between the casket and the assembled crowd. The man, bearded and balding and wearing a suit that had last fit during the Eisenhower administration, played a guitar and was singing something unrecognizable. Joining him in the mysterious hymn was a woman with shoulder-length blonde hair, seated on a stool. Did they just travel with a portable stool? I knew it didn't belong to the funeral home.

Walking over towards Asa, who'd reappeared, I leaned and whispered into his ear.

"Peter and Mary are here but someone forgot to let Paul know about the gig."

He and I agreed that driving the limo for this family had been the result of no one else wanting to do it. He said he'd put in a good word with my dad and maybe I could just drive the deceased from now on, but only in funerals and not to the airport or the crematory.

The chance for that came that same summer when Wayman Price died. He'd lived in a large house in the Old Point section downtown. The houses there were largely built in the 1800's. As a result, many of them had faulty electrical wiring or no central heating and air and overlooked streets paved just wide enough for horses to pass.

My dad had picked me up from our house in the hearse to go get Mr. Price from his home. It was another hot afternoon and Dad always preferred to pick up the recently deceased with another person. When we pulled up to the house, I could see that it was definitely a two-person job, though I was soon to learn I hadn't been promoted to be the face of the company yet.

"Stay out here while I go in," he said, taking the empty stretcher from the back of the hearse in with him.

I could only stand awkwardly on the front steps and look into the windows of the magnificent house, like a gardener too dirty to come inside but too polite to be left sitting on a tree stump. I could see the oil painting over the fireplace and the wooden chairs placed carefully around the table in the dining room. It must have been a nice place to live, let alone die.

It was towards the back end of the oldest, most historic neighborhood in Beaufort. You couldn't walk down the street without Spanish moss hitting you in the head from one of the low hanging oaks. The houses were close together but this one was another majestic house among many.

As the front doors opened again, I saw my dad come walking out with who I assumed was Mrs. Price.

"Grab the end of this," he said, gesturing to the now-filled stretcher with a sheet completely covering it.

There's no pressure quite like handling a stretcher with a respected community member's body on it and navigating the steep, treacherous front steps while his widow looks on. Naturally I walked down backwards, allowing my dad the ability to walk down normally and keep an eye on things from above me. He was a stickler for doing even the simplest tasks with dignity, and taking the body of a person who was alive just hours ago out of their home and into the back of a hearse required the ultimate attention to detail. When I reached the bottom of the stairs I noticed the sheet had wrinkled near the bottom of the stretcher, which my dad quickly smoothed out while shooting me a glance that let me know he thought it was my fault it had gotten out of place.

Still, he trusted me enough to drive the hearse with Mr. Price's body two days later from the funeral home to the funeral service at St. Peter's Catholic Church on Lady's Island. It was a quiet ride and the sun broke out in the sky just as we - Mr. Price and I - reached the apex of the Woods Bridge downtown. It felt like there was a brief moment when it was just our hearse on the bridge and only dolphins in the water and birds in the sky as we headed towards his final service of remembrance.

Later, when the funeral was over and I needed to drive the hearse back over the bridge to the cemetery where Mr. Price would be buried, I abruptly pulled out from the church parking lot into traffic at what I thought was the police officer's instruction. I saw him wave, but I left without the limo or the rest of the funeral cortege behind me.

At the same time I noticed the officer directing traffic around me, I saw my dad come running out into the median where I had pulled. For every other driver on the road, it must have been a comic scene to see a hearse stalled in the middle of traffic while a tall, dark-suited undertaker came out and yelled at the driver. Thankfully, poor Mr. Price was spared the indignity of hearing the ass-chewing I got.

Perhaps as a direct result of my inability to drive either a hearse or a limousine in a funeral, the next summer I was asked to participate in something a little more up my alley. It was also something any random idiot could have done without screwing up too bad.

By then I was about to start my senior year of high school and was working at the local Sears unloading trailers full of appliances and lawn and garden equipment and reloading them into the backs of pickups when they became customer purchases. As that was a six day-a-week job, my only time to work at the funeral home was on my "off" days.

In the alcove of the garage of the funeral home - still tantalizingly close to both the limousine and the hearse - were two large filing cabinets. In those cabinets were folders containing files of Coroner's Office cases that dated back to the 1930's. Since that time there had only been three coroners for Beaufort County: Roger Pinckney IX, Roger Pinckney X and my dad.

What was asked of me was to stay in the little alcove (metal folding chair provided for comfort) and organize the files by years and transfer them into boxes for eventual placement in the county's fireproof records building.

On the surface it seemed easy enough. Take the file folders and place them chronologically into the provided boxes. The first few were a breeze. All of the 1930's, for instance, fit into one third of one box. I placed a divider in and was able to get all of the 1940's files into the same box. This was going to be a breeze!

What I didn't account for was how distracting some of the cases would be to read.

In the case files of the from the 1940's, for instance, I read of a "negro girl struck by lightning" on St. Helena, a rare case in any decade. Of course, reading the word "negro" made me shudder, as out of date at the time as the cursive handwriting in which it was written.

As I moved through the years one thing became obvious - the stacks of paperwork were becoming indefinitely larger. Where one entire decade could once fit into one half of a box, as I moved from the 1980's into the 1990's, I could no longer even fit one year of files into one box.

Somewhere in the 1980's, Beaufort had been "discovered" by Hollywood and others on the Southern Living subscription list. If you make the "Most Charming Small Town in America" list once or twice, people will want to come check you out for themselves.

As retirement communities sprang up all over the county as far as Hilton Head and Bluffton clear up through Dataw and Fripp Island, the population of the county more than doubled in the 20 years between 1980 and 2000. With a population increase came the natural increase in deaths that were not always natural.

Remember that a coroner only has to investigate deaths that don't occur naturally at home or in a hospital. They're called to the scene of murders and drownings and vehicle accidents and when tractors roll over people mistakenly or a second floor porch collapses with someone on it. Yes, those are tragically real. So no, there wasn't an uptick in the crime rate in Beaufort per capita, just more people here to make bad choices.

More coroner cases equals more paperwork, but I started to lose interest in poring over every file looking for an interesting manner of death. Occasionally a photograph would fall out of a file and I'd have to pick it up to look at it. Once you've seen bodies lying in a freezer you can't really unsee it. If you've seen one self-inflicted gunshot wound, you've seen them all.

They're all somewhat disturbing as they're all an unnatural way to die by definition. As Dr. Ray Kearns, a Beaufort chiropractor used to say (to the great delight of my grandmother, his neighbor and friend), all he wanted at the end of life was to "wake up dead." That can't happen for us all, and despite the depressing nature of categorizing and boxing up old case files and seeing the names of people grow exponentially through the years, focusing on getting the job done as required was the main goal. I guess that's what keeps a coroner himself going strong without going nuts.

It took a good two or three weekends to finish the job, working as slowly as I did. When I finally loaded the last box into the bed of my truck, I drove out of the funeral home parking lot towards the fireproof county building off of Depot Road with the knowledge that I'd finally found something I could do. I'm not saying it's why I eventually became a librarian, but being around historical information that needed to be classified did hit something within me. Working alone in my own corner of the garage, away from other humans (living or dead) was preferable to driving a limo or a hearse or a tractor.

That much I'd learned the hard way, and I can thank my dad for that.

CHAPTER V.

It's rare that you meet other people who grew up in similar circumstances as you when you grew up in the funeral business that you rejected as an adult. Sure, military brats can recognize each other in every back alley in America, and ministers' kids always recognize each other at the therapist's, but when I met Justin Hardy, whose dad still runs a funeral home in Georgia, I knew I'd met someone who could relate.

I teach with Justin's wife, Justine (not a joke name), and Justin himself is the Land and Wildlife Manager at Palmetto Bluff in Bluffton, SC. We have a lot in common, even if he's got an air of coolness I'll never possess. I asked him a few questions to help break up this book and give a different perspective. Not everyone has the same experience, and Justin seems to be more serious and introspective - a nice change of pace from my own absurdities. He kindly and graciously took time away from his family and his time in the beauty of nature to answer.

1. When did you first realize your dad did something "different" or unique for a living?

Daddy has held a lot of "different" jobs. He's been a train engineer. He owned a candy company for a while. He has been in and out of the funeral business all his life though. He built his own funeral home shortly after I graduated high school. I don't know that I ever had a realization or epiphany that his job was odd or different. It never seemed strange to me. It was just a part of life. Ironic?

2. Did he also make you work there for free because it's the "family business?"

I worked at the funeral home off and on but I was fortunate enough to always get paid.

3. Did you ever get any kind of weird questions about what your dad did for a living while growing up?

Always! I still get questions. The questions are generally about the embalming process. What do they stuff you with? Do they suck out your guts? I've also been asked about the most gruesome things I've seen. I can't answer most of these questions because Daddy kept me away from the "nitty gritty". My role at the funeral home involved moving flower arrangements, washing cars, yard work, vacuuming, that sort of thing. If I could answer the questions, I wouldn't anyway out of respect for the deceased.

4. Do any incidents stand out in your memory - mishaps at funerals, etc.?

Dad keeps his business wired tight and he has an eye for detail. Things generally ran smooth and that's important.

5. When did you decide a career as a funeral director wasn't for you?

Before graduating high school, I thought I would go into the business. It was an economy-proof business and, at that time, the economy was in the dump. Daddy urged me to get a degree in something else as a fall back in case the funeral business wasn't for me. Somewhere between 18 and 21, I realized I wasn't cut out for the business (not the other way around). I don't believe that I have the appropriate personality. It takes a special type of person to be a good funeral director. My dad fits the mold. My older sister does as well and she has entered the business.

6. Anything else you'd like to add? Speak now or...you know the drill.

Funeral directors who are successful and remain in the business (based on directors I've personally met) typically have a strong religious faith. Maybe it helps with coping with the morbidity of their business. It definitely helps when working with the survivors. Funerals, if we are being honest, are not for the one who has passed. They're for the survivors. My dad and sister are both devout Methodist Christians and always have been. My faith isn't on par with theirs.

Also, there is an undefined air that makes a good "funeral man." It's something like a somber sociability. It's a confidence that you don't notice if you aren't looking for it. Good directors are able to effectively work with people who are really not in the mood to talk or make decisions and are generally having one of the worst weeks of their lives. I'm not good in these types of situations. I can barely even come up with words to describe whatever the trait actually is. I just know I don't have much of it.

My own personality has led me into a workplace where I'm much more comfortable. I'm a land and wildlife manager. I work with deer and turkeys and snakes and bugs and trees and it suits me well. My dad oozes the "funeral man" personality. People who are in their worst hours look to him for guidance and that's pretty special. I respect him immeasurably.

PHOTO INSERT

Dad and Mom in 1970, the year after they moved (back) to
Beaufort.

My dad holding my sister, Shelley, while his best friend Ed Duryea
holds his daughter, Katy, on his shoulders.

Dad in his real estate office during what I call his "Telemundo" phase of not shaving the awful mustache.

Dad during a Water Festival parade in Beaufort. He'd been the Commodore of the 1975 Festival. The little girl with the blond curls is me. I'm a boy.

My sister and me finding fun with boxes at the back of Dad's real estate office. Not nearly as exciting as climbing into caskets but it'll do in a pinch.

Whenever a group in dark suits is gathered...it's probably a funeral home staff (or possibly members of the Gambino crime family). Funeral home staff in the 1980's looked exactly like this, because that's who they were. Dad is on the far right. His right-hand man, Asa Godowns, is on the bottom step at the front. Behind him, in the middle with white hair, is my granddad Cecil Reames, my true temperamental ancestor. He worked for dad briefly after his retirement from Kinghorn Building Supply.

Already ill at ease during the dedication of the funeral home chapel. Am I handing out programs or working as some sort of weird pastel carnival barker?

Is there anything more "80's" than this photo? Metal swing set. Plaid shorts. White socks with the Converse shoes. Dale Murphy-era Braves hat. Snapper lawn mower. Got it all covered.

One of Dad's favorite places - behind the mic and in front of the
camera. Here he's speaking at a fundraising event downtown on
behalf of (former) SC Governor Carroll Campbell.

Another favorite spot - Waterfront Park emceeing a Water Festival
event.

Sworn in for a third term as coroner (1989) by friend, neighbor and Beaufort County Clerk-of-Court Henry Jackson.

On the phone in his office at the funeral home after another
successful re-election in 1992. Yes, he's as happy as he seems.

A remnant from the 1996 re-election campaign.

My 15th birthday party at Bay Cafe and Ice Cream, which Dad owned and where I worked with this bevy of beauties. I had a massive, unrequited crush on one of them, Julie. I won't tell you which one she is but she's smiling.

Requisite "dad" photo of him at his grill. You can't see his all-white
New Balance shoes. Summer of 1999, around the time he was
cooking up a plan to offer free funerals for drunk drivers on New
Year's Eve.

If there's one thing my dad and I shared, it was a genuine ease with and love for children of all shapes and sizes. Here he's with my cousin's son, Tyler, who would later be the ringbearer at my wedding.

Dad with my wife, Leigh, about a year before she made the mistake of marrying me.

With four of his six grandchildren (Mabrey, Carter, Clara and
Lukas) at his and my mom's 40th wedding anniversary party.
(2008)

Helping my older son, Lukas, put the stuffed cardinal on top of the Christmas tree. Behind them you can make out my teeth and my right eye.

Holding my nephew, Tillman, at (what else?) a funeral.

Thanks to Mike Fleischbein for capturing what I'm sure was a captivating Sea Island Rotary meeting.

My youngest, Reames, at my dad's grave on Christmas Day, 2018. (It's not a tradition to visit graves at Christmas, we were just killing time while the rest of the family was at a church service).

Curt Copeland (1945-2010)

CHAPTER VI.

Though the coroner is an elected position in South Carolina and there's no way to liberally or conservatively fill out a death certificate, it's a public service position that doesn't get a lot of thanks. Dad was sued and taken to trial in his role as coroner, cases which you can find online, but because of the litigious society in which we live I'm prevented from writing about.

I will say that if there were a hypothetical situation where a single-vehicle accident resulted in a death and law required an autopsy, a coroner who determined the body's condition prevented bone marrow from being drawn without great difficulty, well, that coroner probably did what he thought best at the time.

In reality, my dad's own experience as an elected coroner for Beaufort County did, oddly enough, begin with controversy.

First elected as a Democrat in 1980, he ran again as a Republican in 1984 after switching parties because it was starting to get easier to be elected Republican in the South. Though there is no way to fill out a death certificate conservatively or liberally, getting elected to the office meant holding sway over the people who would vote you in. Beaufort rode the Reagan wave into a consistently Republican tidal pool by the 1990's. Dad raised me and my sister, however, to think for ourselves with politics. His own voting record and beliefs were logical for someone who was a member of both parties. That's the best way to sum it up.

The coroner's job - for so long in Beaufort County held by a member of the Pinckney family - was a natural extension of his abilities and talents. It is now, as always, described as a job "responsible for investigating all suspicious, violent, sudden and unexpected deaths which occur in Beaufort County from Hilton Head Island to Fripp Island, including the cities of Beaufort, Bluffton, Port Royal, Hilton Head and a part of Yemassee. This includes all deaths by homicide, suicide, accident, and natural deaths which occur outside a hospital or within the first 24 hours of arrival at the hospital or an invasive procedure."

When he ran for coroner in 1980, he was also running a real estate company and had sold his first funeral home because it wasn't making much money at the time.

"I'm out of the funeral business but it's still in me. There's something gratifying about helping people in times of their greatest need," he told *The Beaufort Gazette.*

Still, by his first full year in office he was providing stories for that same paper by exceeding his county budget appropriation. The lede of one story said "death has gotten a step ahead of the coroner." Apparently there were an unusual amount of autopsies performed that year for suspicious deaths. Anticipating the shortfall, he had asked the county council for a $2500 increase to cover the costs.

"If I'm going to sign the death certificate, I want a conclusion to why the person died," he said in the article.

Of course, the increase in autopsies went along with the population boom that started around that same time.

By 1984, puff pieces were being written about the local "Jack Of All Trades" who was still in real estate, about to open another funeral home and still the now-properly-budgeted coroner. He'd already made the paper for playing tic-tac-toe during a school board meeting with a fellow board (bored?) member, so any press after that was bound to be flattering.

It was also the same year he made it into a national radio story by Dr. Norman Vincent Peale because of happenstance.

Coming back from my sister's dance recital in Savannah (did no one care that I, too, had to suffer in that audience?), we were crossing the Broad River Bridge when Dad noticed traffic had slowed to a halt. There was a commotion up ahead on the bridge over to the right side, so Dad jumped out of the car and ran over.

A marine had been fishing on the left side of the bridge on the catwalk, so when he surreptitiously jumped down on the other side expecting there to be a catwalk there, too, he probably surprised himself when the saltwater went up his nostril.

Some fishing companions heard him hit the water and started to wave down traffic. Once Dad got there and some of the crowd realized he was the coroner - with access to emergency radio - they waved him over to take a look.

Dad called for backup and before long emergency workers and a young Marine (those guys are everywhere!) were down in the marsh helping get the young man back up out of the current and into safety.

After being picked up, the fisherman told The Beaufort Gazette "the good Lord was looking after me, or I wouldn't be here."

Dad enjoyed the thrill of being part of a rescue, for once, and not just on the scene of a rescue attempt gone wrong.

Being coroner would, indeed, prove to be his most exciting job, even if it was later called "part time" by another member of county council in yet another budget dispute.

As the son of the coroner, it was really fun to hold his badge and take it around without him knowing so I could pretend to arrest people. That was about where the fun ended, however.

The badge itself was a reminder to him that he was always on-call, not a necessarily part-time thing. It allowed him access to a radio siren and detachable blue light, as well, which he used on occasion to pull over speeding drivers. "Do you have any idea how fast you were going, or do you know what I do for a living?" he would ask. Part of his rhetorical approach was to always ask a question first to get to his point later. He would tell people he wanted all their encounters with him to be while they were still alive.

There were several Christmas mornings where we waited to open presents because he'd been out early in the morning to deal with an unexpected death. As whiny as we were about waiting, it was always a worse Christmas for someone else when my dad had to go to work.

My sister recalls being in the car with him after he'd picked her up from dance lessons - a normal thing for a working dad to do - when he heard a call on the radio about a suspect fleeing the scene of a robbery. He and my sister were near enough to the scene that he thought he'd flip on his blue lights and help out. He loved playing that role of law-enforcement helper.

Taking the car towards where the suspect was fleeing, he heard the police on the radio talk about a possible roadblock. He swung his own Crown Victoria across the road and turned on his siren. Had the car come through, it would have hit my sister in the passenger side. Rather than realizing this, however, he backed the car up out of the road when it hit him that it wasn't a county vehicle.

"Oh yeah," he said aloud. "I'm the one paying for this car."

My sister remembers another incident of being in the car with him when he was called to the scene of a drowning on Hilton Head. Hanging her head in amazement, she saw that the drowning had occurred inside of a rowboat that had filled with rainwater. A man had left the bar across the street and literally stumbled into the boat next to the woods. He was too drunk to get himself out of the way when water started filling his lungs.

I was with my parents and their friends Ed and Cindy Duryea one Sunday evening when we'd been out to look at my uncle's house, then under construction. They all decided to leave there and head to dinner at Shoney's. I know. Try to contain the jealousy stemming from that sentence.

Since we were in two cars, I decided to ride with Ed and Cindy and their son, my friend Huntley. We were following my dad over the bridge from Lady's Island when we noticed he, himself, was following a car that was swerving. Before I knew it, Dad had his blue lights on and we were in hot pursuit in the backup car. Actually, it was a Dodge van we were riding in, but it had no trouble playing its part in this odd parade of drunk driver followed by coroner's car closely tailed by family friend.

The car finally pulled over in the parking lot of a Church's Chicken. Like Shoney's, Church's is anachronism now that exists only in mostly unpleasant memories.

When the driver, a man in jeans and a t-shirt, got out of the car, he dashed towards the door of the restaurant, but police who had already arrived had told Church's employees to lock the door. Dad had obviously radioed in and told them what was happening. From the backseat of the van, Huntley and I watched as the man, frustrated by the locked door, turned around and whaled on a police officer.

Another officer quickly threw the man against the wall of the restaurant while Dad grabbed a nightstick from the first officer and hit the man on the head with what can only be described as the most tentative swing ever taken by someone not named Bob Uecker. He tapped the man on the head, again and again, while other officers arrived on the scene to help subdue him.

It was almost as if Dad was afraid to strike hard enough to cause permanent damage, but didn't want to stand around doing nothing. It looked like he was swatting at a palmetto bug that he wasn't sure was going to fly at him or not.

I asked Ed and Cindy why the first officer who'd been hit was now standing against the patrol car with his arms holding up his body to keep it from what looked like complete collapse.

"He just...got the wind knocked out of him," is how Ed politely put it.

My sister was somehow not with us during that incident, but we do both remember being in the car when Dad had picked us up from school and rerouted towards the scene of a house fire on St. Helena. The charred bodies that were being loaded onto the stretcher and the smell of burned flesh, even with the windows rolled up, is not something easy to forget.

We both also have a million "do you remember that time?" kind of stories about being with Dad when he suddenly had to go "on duty" and we had to go along and be as quiet and out-of-the-way as possible, including the time the whole family - my grandparents included - sat in my dad's car while he was called to the scene of a murder-suicide on Hilton Head. On a rainy Saturday, just hours - maybe even minutes - after my mom had been presented the Teacher-of-the-Year award for the school district. What had been a celebratory occasion for my mom turned into another day at the office for my dad, and we were all at work with him, watching the raindrops slide their way up his windshield as blue lights circled the perimeter.

It was never fun, but it could have always been worse. We weren't the ones being visited by the coroner, after all.

No, what struck us as the most defining difference growing up was the dinner conversations we were exposed to some nights. It was difficult eating meatloaf, period, but even more difficult eating it while discussing physician-assisted suicide.

A case on Fripp Island where a woman helped her terminally ill mother end her life led to some great debate at dinner time. While Dad wanted to abide by the laws of the time in punishing the daughter for slowly injecting her elderly mother with an overdose of medication, he also understood the need to end suffering. No other kids in my class knew Dr. Jack Kevorkian from Doogie Howser, MD, but I know I formed an opinion on euthanasia at an awfully young age.

Gang-related activity? Yeah, probably not a hot topic at the table for the family of a Radio Shack salesperson, but when it resulted in the death of a child, it became a week-long discussion in our house exploring culture and class divisions.

Though I was older when Franciso Belman died, I remember his death affected Dad because, like so many, it was avoidable.

As a 14-year-old student at McCracken Middle School in Bluffton, Belman was trying to join a Latin mafia gang, as much as middle school students can create one of those, when he was told to participate in an initiation ceremony. This initiation involved being punched in the chest multiple times out of view of the teachers or administrators. In the school bathroom, an awful place to take your last breath, the poor kid was punched one too many times.

After collapsing and convulsing, gang members tried to revive him before summoning adults. Paramedics were called, of course, but also unable to get his heart back into rhythm. His resulting vegetative state lasted roughly two months before he died.

When he did, the two boys who admitted to punching him were charged with involuntary manslaughter and put on probation.

"For all intents and purposes, he was sent home to die," Dad told The Island Packet at the time.

It raised multiple questions at the time, including doubts about the prevalence of Latin gangs in the Lowcountry, the oversight of school officials during the school day, even the need for boys to fit in by risking violence for the sake of friendship.

When a financial settlement was reached with the county, it raised an even more pressing question - how much was a young life actually worth? Could you even put a value on that?

The answers to all of those, of course, are almost rhetorical in that they can be debated and quantified and never concluded.

Dad was bothered that Belman had to die for wanting to be a part of something. He felt just as bad for the two boys who'd have what equated to murder on their consciences at an age when you couldn't really comprehend weighty issues.

It also happened right around the advent of internet message boards and comment sections of articles, so there was some insensitivity in the community.

"Sooo... the newest gang recruit died during his initiation ceremony," someone anonymously wrote. "Am I supposed to mourn? Spare me the tears. One less danger to our neighborhoods has been self terminated. Good riddance."

This was followed by another commenter stating "I'm sad this kid died - he didn't deserve it. But Lord, something called 'Latin Mafia' can't be good. These kids want so bad to be accepted, they will die for it."

Honestly it's good that message boards hadn't existed during Dad's earlier career when he called for Coroner's Inquests quite often to help determine the cause of death in a questionable situation.

According to the S.C. Code of Laws, Section 17-7-20, "whenever a body is found dead and an investigation or inquest is deemed advisable the coroner or the magistrate acting as coroner, as the case may be, shall go to the body and examine the witnesses most likely to be able to explain the cause of death, take their testimony in writing and decide for himself whether there ought to be a trial or whether blame probably attaches to any living person for death, and if so and he shall receive the written request, if any, he shall proceed to summon a jury and hold a formal inquest as required by law."

To say Dad used a liberal interpretation of this in enacting his duties is an understatement.

He held inquests several times to help determine, by jury, who was at fault in vehicular accidents. Who was responsible for a murder with multiple suspects? Who was at fault when a trucker claimed his brakes didn't work and he killed another driver?

In 1987, an inquest went the opposite way of its intent, at least for my dad.

"Murder charge squashed; coroner 'totally shocked'" said the headline in the Beaufort Gazette.

Apparently an 18-year-old woman had given her older brother the holiday gift of a bullet to the head in 1986. Apparently the older brother had flashed a knife at some point early Christmas morning, threateningly and violently, and wasn't exactly the kind of guy a ton of people would miss had he packed up and moved west. Apparently the multiple witnesses at the home that night told differing stories to investigators, so Dad had them all thrown in jail that night until they could get their story straight.

The story was that during a scuffle either the young man, at 19 only one-year older than his sister, shot himself when the gun accidentally went off against his skull, or his sister shot him without meaning it to be fatal. Either way, he was gone.

Dad ordered a jury of six people to "determine if the victim had come to death by accident or by felony, and if by felony, who were the principles and who were the accessories."

After hearing from all witnesses at the home during the shooting, which included the siblings' parents, other brother and respective boyfriend and girlfriend, the jury determined the sister had done the shooting. She was then charged with murder based on their recommendation.

Later, however, a circuit judge threw out the murder charge and gave the sister the lesser count of involuntary manslaughter, leading to the infamous headline above.

"At worst it was self-defense and at best it was an accident," said the judge at the time.

"In six years, this is the first time I've vehemently disagreed," Dad's prepared responsive statement read. "It appears the judge condones the taking of a life by another because the decedent was a 'bad' guy and yet the courts spend years and thousands of dollars in the appeals process before an execution takes place. I suppose the moral of the story is that it is fine to kill someone if you can justify to the judge the character of the person you kill."

So yes, sometimes it is a coroner's place to get involved in a morally ambiguous situation involving the circumstances of a death that is repeated in newspapers around the county. Of course, his statement received a rejoinder from the family of the deceased and his sister.

"In regards to the statements that were written in the paper from Curt Copeland: You were not at our home when this happened, you do not know what caused it, what led to the end," they wrote in a published letter-to-the-editor of the Beaufort Gazette. "You can have and say all the opinions you like but it was still an accident. Accidents do happen. Unfortunately our son paid for it… you are not God….you never asked us one question that night as to what happened or how. You were too busy putting a family and our friends in jail."

So there you have it. A controversial and public case that played out with absolutely no winners.

Inquests certainly became less popular over time and I'm not sure if this case and the way it played out had anything to do with it, but an accidental death at a family home where the coroner can't get good answers as to how it happened wasn't common.

Plane crashes were also a relatively uncommon occurrence for Beaufort. Relatively. It's not exactly the Bermuda Triangle of the airspace in the Lowcountry, but it isn't as rare as you might think. For the record, I don't think the Illuminati is responsible for any of it.

In the late 1980's, one small private plane traveling north from Tampa Bay lost radar contact about 13 miles southeast of Hilton Head, but it was only when fisherman recovered the body of one of the plane's passengers and took her to Hilton Head Hospital in a vain attempt to save her was it truly known that the plane had gone down in the ocean.

Not too long after that another plane, suffering from what the National Transportation Safety Board called a mid-air explosion, downed in Battery Creek right outside the view of a residential neighborhood. Wreckage from that was recovered for weeks in the marshes of the creeks and rivers.

There were others through the years-a failed takeoff at Hilton Head Airport that crash landed on Highway 278, killing the couple onboard-but none as terrible in the collective public memory in Beaufort as the death of the Blue Angel pilot, Lt. Commander Kevin Davis.

If you don't know the Blue Angels, they're kind of the elite pilot crew of the US Navy. Also, if you don't know the Blue Angels, what kind of life are you even living?

They perform at air shows at various military bases throughout the country, and in 2007 they were back at Marine Corps Air Station Beaufort putting on a show for thousands in the warm April afternoon.

After finishing the stunt portion of the show and descending into their final turns before the landing pattern, the plane took a dive as Lt. Commander Davis became disoriented by the G-forces involved in the turn. He lost both consciousness and control of the plane. However, by providence or good luck or maybe some sort of knowledge and skill on his part before he lost consciousness, the plane went down near a tree line in a residential neighborhood outside of the base.

There were thousands of dollars in damage, of course, but only one fatality.

Instead of being at the air show that day, I had chosen to be at the competing Crab Festival in Port Royal. It's not that I didn't like air shows (I don't). I wasn't even avoiding crowds (I was). I just can't handle the noise of the engines that close. I didn't even like fireworks shows as a child.

Once the plane went down, however, word spread quickly among the crowd at the crab festival. You've never seen so many people quietly leave a party without knowing exactly why or what to do, but the pall was over the entire crowd and it was palpable.

My sister and her family had been at the air show that day and knew immediately something very wrong had happened. The plume of smoke coming from the trees across the highway soon confirmed it. They were stuck for hours as emergency crews cleared the site before any of the traffic could be released.

My mom had been at the funeral home with my dad helping him with a visitation when he got the call. She remembers him literally running to his car and peeling out of the funeral home driveway to get to the air station.

That's probably something he learned from his predecessor Roger Pinckney - the need for taking command of a death scene. There would be EMS workers there already, in addition to firemen, policemen, military personnel, etc. What they would need is someone to coordinate the efforts and try to preserve the accident site as best as possible.

Of course, when something like this happens it becomes "Breaking News" on CNN and Fox, even in a post-9/11 world. I went home and watched the live footage of what was occurring just minutes from my house on Lady's Island, the smoke clouds visible from the bridge as well as my television.

Dad, quoted in national and international news sources, could only describe the crash and its circumstances as "horrific."

It was an amazingly succinct thought for someone who enjoyed the occasional media attention and used the office to raise awareness of certain issues.

He was always a proponent of widening any kind of road in any area. It was less about his concern for the South Carolina Highway Department having continual work and more about alleviating traffic and therefore lessening traffic-related deaths.

In his mind those kinds were always avoidable. He never had an accurate count of murders or suicides or plane crashes in the Lowcountry, but he could tell you how many people were killed on Highway 17 in 1994. (I don't know the number. I said he could tell you, not me).

His most famous publicity stunt to bring attention to driving hazards was his 1999 offer of a free funeral to anyone willing to sign a statement with him saying they were planning to drink and drive on New Year's Eve. Anyone stupid enough to sign it and actually follow through would receive a free embalming and casket.

Of course I lived through the notoriety of that one, but for other years of my dad being coroner I had to rely on my mom's memory and the archives she kept. Many times Dad couldn't talk about an investigation until it was complete. Sometimes we didn't know what he was going through mentally because he couldn't legally say.

What we have looking back on a 28-year career as coroner for a growing county is a few cases that stick out, either for how unusual they were or how they mentally tormented him. No human is immune to the anguish of an accidental or purposeful death, even if you deal in it for a living.

Sometimes, after a flooding rain or a hurricane, caskets become dislodged from their surroundings under the earth. This is a hazard of dying in a place surrounded by the Atlantic Ocean and its tributaries. If they're lucky, they'll only float several hundred feet downriver before being recovered and reburied. That's a "natural" exhumation.

Intentional exhumations, by definition, are arduous. It's not only difficult to literally dig up a casket and perform the proper procedures on a body that's been placed inside of it for however long, it's also difficult on surviving family members to relive the death of their loved one.

For years whenever my family drove by a roadside church on the way to Savannah, we would remember that it was the church where the former pastor was rumored to have killed his wife. Though she had died in a hospital from swelling on the brain that overwhelmed her, the rumors were so persistent that Dad was duly obliged to exhume the body to have more testing done. The tests, performed by a forensic pathologist, were inconclusive at best, but not enough to charge anyone with wrongdoing. In a small town, however, the rumors will chase you into the next state.

Another thing that happens in a small town is that you sometimes have to deal, as a public official, with situations involving people you or your family know.

Tragically, my sister's graduating class at Beaufort High School had experienced the most random and unexpected deaths of four classmates for perhaps any group of students who grew up together. By 1992 they'd lost a classmate to a drowning on Hunting Island, another to skin cancer and yet another to encephalitis from a mosquito bite.

Yes, we live surrounded by water so the idea of a drowning is an unfortunate but not altogether rare occurrence. Sun and mosquitoes go hand-in-hand here as well, even if you don't expect either of them to take your life. You don't expect parents to outlive children, either, but that also happens from time to time.

What happened to the fourth classmate, Bruce Edgerly, is something so rare that it almost never happens at all.

Edgerly was practicing with the rest of the Beaufort High Baseball team on the field at the school one afternoon when he didn't hear the coach call his name. As an infielder, Edgerly was used to fielding balls hit by the coaches and turning to throw to first base. This time, however, his attention was elsewhere as when the ball was hit.

He may or may not have seen or felt it coming. Some of his teammates surely did. The crows that used to fly over the field may have sensed it, and probably some of the gnats that stirred in the infield dirt felt time stand still. No doubt the coach who hit the ball immediately wished he could outrun it and catch it himself.

Regardless, when the line drive hit Edgerly's chest it stopped his heart cold. The thud that hit his arteries and valves was comparable to the sound of his body hitting the ground. It all happened around the same time.

"It knocked his heart out of sync, they were never able to revive him."

That was a quote from my dad that they ran under the story in the Weekly World News, a tabloid that published sensationally fictionalized stories.

Unfortunately this story was too real, and when my sister got home that evening and word had already spread about what happened in the days before texting, she and a friend walked around outside in silence, unable to give voice to the incomprehensible.

Dad's job as coroner had already taken him from the hospital to the Edgerly home, but his job as a dad wasn't done, as he had to try to comfort my sister and her friend in the way he'd been trained to deal with unexpected death.

What he'd not been trained enough in was how to deal with the emotional impact of the death of children. I remember nothing shaking him quite as much as the death of young Kimi Slattery in 1998.

I was in high school and already used to having as little interaction with my parents as a teenager could get away with, but this case made my dad shut down for a while to deal with it as best he could.

A case involving the murder of a child was thankfully rare but hopelessly incomprehensible. Trying to investigate it was where Dad earned his "part-time" income.

Though the child, a seven-year-old girl under the care of her mother's boyfriend that chilly February night, wouldn't be pronounced dead until almost midnight at Beaufort Memorial Hospital, the autopsy placed her actual death hours earlier.

The child, Kimi, was in bed when her mother came back home from her shift at a fast food restaurant. The mother's boyfriend, a man named Roy Dean White, told her that Kimi was in bed and should be checked on.

What her mother found was that her little girl was propped up in bed, surrounded by stuffed animals, with foam around her mouth and blood dried in her nose, not to mention pooled on her lower half.

Her mother immediately called 911 while neighbors came over to administer CPR. It was all in vain, of course, and White probably knew it would be.

Dad issued a Coroner's Warrant to hold White in jail while a cause of death was determined.

When the autopsy subsequently revealed that asphyxia as part of a sexual assault was the cause of death, there were not many words that could be offered as an explanation.

"The senseless, brutal, horrible death of this sweet little girl was a result of something not natural," was all my dad could tell the press at the time.

He brought it home with him in that he didn't talk about it for weeks. When he did he would only say that he couldn't stop dreaming about it, even if it was more of a nightmare. I noticed that when he fell asleep on the couch at night for a couple of weeks afterwards, he would awaken with a sudden jump and be unable to fall back asleep easily. All the murder-scene photos, investigative interviews and autopsy reports would eventually get to even the most sane human being, so Dad was no different, and his mood greatly affected ours in the house.

It's difficult, even reading this now, to believe that evil like this exists around us. In our reverie for the salt water and sunshine and palmetto trees that surround our centuries-old homes, we forget that there's a darker side to humanity that sometimes surfs and skis and shops right alongside us. Dad could never escape that reality because he could never turn away from the result when that evil is unleashed.

Yes, they put Roy Dean White away, but not forever. When he was out of prison in 2012 and celebrating in a local restaurant, Kimi's father saw him and left the restaurant in disgust. Months later he took his own life, unable to comprehend how his daughter's killer was able to walk free while Kimi never again would.

It's maybe more of an indictment of the justice system than anything else, but dealing with child-murders was not terribly different, in Dad's mind, than dealing with people who shoot police officers.

There had already been an incident in 1995 when a mentally disturbed man shot a Beaufort County Sheriff's Deputy and a Port Royal Police Officer during a standoff at the Driftwood Campground near Gray's Hill. Both officers survived the shots fired at them by Douglas Click.

Click had already been in and out of mental hospitals when he was pulled over for reckless driving. Instead of acquiescing, he grabbed a shotgun and jumped onto the roof of his car. He fired and hit one deputy in the eye (which caused the loss of vision in the eye) and another in the forehead. They managed to subdue Click with pepper spray and successfully arrested him.

Four years later Click killed himself in the Kmart parking lot, and dad spent the better part of a day cordoning off the very public scene and trying to notify the next of kin. Deputies at the scene weighed the morality of a man who'd taken his own life after trying to take the lives of two fellow policemen.

Though both of those officers lived through their incident, a similar one in 2002 changed Beaufort forever.

In the late afternoon of a random February day in 2002, two deputies received a call about a domestic disturbance and a woman possibly being held against her will at a home in Burton. Tucked behind a mostly wooded road near the Broad River Bridge was a blue mobile home, covered by the fading sunlight of winter and the bare foliage of the trees.

When Beaufort County Sheriff's Deputies Dana Tate and AJ Coursen arrived at the scene, it took them close to twenty minutes to determine what was going on inside the house. They eventually entered the house with guns drawn. What happened next was described as a closeted ambush by their suspect, Tyree Roberts, though Roberts himself later told investigators that the officers shot him first.

The end result, however, was that Roberts shot Tate and Coursen a half-dozen times or more, each.

Tate was the one who likely got Roberts in return fire, but the wound was not fatal and Roberts escaped from the mobile home, moving past the still bodies of the officers as he escaped.

As Roberts left the house he tried to tell the woman who was being held to follow him, but she refused. She'd had a baby with Roberts, but she wanted no more of what was going on that day.

He instead called his wife from his cell phone while on the move and met her near a small bridge close by. She was the one whom investigators determined had tried to aid in his failed escape. He was ultimately too injured and slow to move far and was eventually captured down in the marsh - along with the AK-47 he had used earlier.

As far as Dad was concerned, it was cut and dry. The hardest job he had was telling Mrs. Tate and Mrs. Coursen that their husbands would not be home that night.

In the subsequent court trial, it had taken jurors mere minutes to find Roberts guilty of murder. A judge sentenced him to death, but appeals filed on his behalf have, to this day, kept him alive far longer than his victims. He remains Beaufort County's only inmate on death row.

The story wasn't over for Dad after the trial, either.

Mrs. Coursen had no home church with which to schedule a funeral for her husband. Something like that - when a community needed to mourn two people they may not have even known - required a large, comforting space.

As he often did when theological questions beyond his pay grade were sure to arise, Dad called a pastor from his own church to go with him to the home. He anticipated the thrashing out of widows and widowers against a God that had, in their mind, maybe, taken out His own wrath on them for no specific reason. If Dad knew the survivors of a murder or a suicide or an accidental death had a church home, he would call their pastor for help. If not, he deferred to his own pastor in the hopes that they could provide comfort to the grief-stricken in ways that Dad, himself, couldn't.

He had done it countless times and did it again with Mrs. Coursen, trying to get her access to resources he thought she'd need, whether she thought she would or not. Coursen's funeral was held at The Baptist Church of Beaufort and the iconic image of that day, preserved by the newspaper, was of Sheriff's deputies - black and white - carrying his casket out of the church and down steps just as steep as the tears on their faces.

Part of what Dad did best was provide comfort.

It also didn't matter when or where he could do it.

Being a funeral director and a coroner always set him up for charges of "double-dipping" or influencing a family who had just had a tragic death occur to choose his funeral home. All I know is that he was sensitive enough to this to know better than to have tried it.

A woman on Hilton Head - not a place Dad typically had funeral home clients - who dealt with him as a coroner can testify to this. As Fran Mollica wrote to the editor of The Island Packet in 1997, she unexpectedly lost her grandmother and her aunt in the same automobile accident in September. As she left the parking lot of Beaufort Memorial Hospital after making a phone call to tell her brother the bad news, she was overcome with emotion. The flushing in her face and dizziness in her head caused her to sit on the sidewalk of the hospital in an apparent daze.

"I am not exactly sure where a very compassionate and kind man, all dressed up in a suit, came from," she said. "I heard through my sobs a gentle and caring voice asking me if he could help."

Of course Dad was already there on business, having gone to the ER after the vehicular accident to help determine the cause of death of Mollica's grandmother and aunt. He called for more medical personnel to come and help her off the pavement and into the waiting room.

"I can remember this tall, thin, kind man continuously wiping my face with a cool, wet cloth," she said. "Only after the gentleman was assured that someone was there with me, did he say that he had to excuse himself but to call if he could do anything."

Only when she asked his name did she find out that he was the coroner.

"Of course I knew his name but never would I have expected him to be there with such sincere compassion and concern for a complete stranger."

Then again, Dad never really met a stranger.

CHAPTER VII.

Picture it - Los Angeles - January of 1992. The air is as thick with smog as ever and the veil of the 1980's is still slowly evaporating to reveal the 1990's. The streets around the campus of UCLA are filled with spike-haired punks and random neighborhood Angelenos looking for the next pointed camera.

Over in nearby Burbank, Johnny Carson is in his last season as host of *The Tonight Show* and my family has tickets to a taping of the show. Why we had come to Los Angeles in January is still a mystery to me, but it was in the middle of a several-years period where we took advantage of Dad owning a travel agency. We would also take family vacations and trips to New York, Boston, Las Vegas, San Francisco and many points in between.

The trip to Los Angeles had already included a day at Universal Studios, a walk down the Avenue of the Stars, seeing the handprints outside of Grauman's Chinese Theatre and one of those daylong Star Tours where you go around looking for celebrities but really just seeing their mailboxes. I had managed to see Barbara Eden coming down an escalator at a shopping plaza on Rodeo Drive while my mom was inside a store shopping. If it had been 1966 and the height of Eden's fame as Jeannie in *I Dream of Jeannie* I'm sure it would have been quite the thrill. As it was, it was all I had so far on the trip on which to hang my hat.

The *Tonight Show* experience would change that.

We possessed four VIP tickets to the Carson show courtesy of Mr. Tom Berenger. As a part-time resident of Beaufort, Berenger and my dad had hooked up somehow through what I assume is legal channels. Just kidding, I think it might have been through Dad's work with various charities and Berenger's generosity and that of his then-wife.

At any rate, I'd met him at least once at an airshow and then stood in line behind him at Revco. No, not CVS. Revco. This was 1992, remember, and Berenger was still relatively hot off the successes of movies like *The Big Chill* (filmed in Beaufort), *Platoon, Someone to Watch Over Me, Major League* and *Sniper*. He was yet to do *Gettysburg, Sliver* and the vastly underrated *The Substitute*. Seriously, that film gets a lot of flack but it's pretty watchable.

I knew who he was, certainly, but that day in Revco I didn't understand why it had gotten so silent until the man in front of me in line walked out and the cashier exhaled. What I'd thought was a relatively harmless hobo was, in fact, Berenger in semi-disguise. To get dressed in sweatpants and a fanny pack and wear a hat over large, Unabomber-style sunglasses just to go get some deodorant must have been a burden.

Years later I was at a restaurant in Beaufort celebrating a friend's birthday when someone in our party pointed out that the place was nearly empty.

"Yep, it's just us, the waitress and Tom over there," said my friend, pointing to a patron alone at the bar.

As we left I noticed that it was Tom Berenger, indeed.

But in 1992 he was friends with Johnny and that's all you needed for VIP tickets to the show.

So on a warm January afternoon in Burbank my family and I made our way into the NBC studios for the 5:00 taping.

Then, as now, the late night shows were filmed and edited for a release later that same night at 11:30pm.

My dad had worshiped Carson and his comedy style, that much I knew. Going to sit in the audience was a huge deal for him. At almost 12 years old I had already been taping Saturday Night Live on our VCR for a couple of years and was really into comedy. Letterman was more my style, so it didn't surprise me that Dad and I were not on the same page. Still, Carson had announced his retirement and we were all ready for the experience of the show.

What we weren't ready for was the rule that the studio audience would only consist of those aged 16 and older. My sister, who was less than a month from being 18, had neglected to bring identification with her. I was not even 13 yet, so the option of me staying alone in the lobby or the parking lot and hoping to not get mugged or abducted was definitely discussed. Nothing was really off the table for my dad when it came to Johnny Carson, including throwing a coat over my head and trying to smuggle me in.

As we were trying to decide what to do, my mom started crying in the lobby in front of God and all the other presumed studio audience members who had not failed to read the fine print. Before it became a news item ("Suburban Mom from South Carolina Throws Hissy Fit in Hollywood Studio!"), out of nowhere, a man came up to us and explained that he was an employee of the show who would solve everything if we would just follow him away from the rest of the suddenly frightened crowd.

His name was Kevin Quinn and he was the stage manager and associate producer for the show. My mom might as well have called him Jesus for the miracle he would soon produce.

He offered to go ahead and seat my parents in the audience while he took me and my sister backstage. After seating them, he led us to the floor of the Tonight Show as it looked then, just beside the famous curtains that parted when Johnny came out. We walked by his desk and the chairs for the guests just to the left of it. After going the wrong way through the curtain, our new best friend Kevin led us to the green room, where he offered us all the Coke and M&M's we wanted.

We sat down on a couch next to a little refrigerator in the green room, but all of the energy around us seemed to be happening in rooms down the hallway. Sensing this, Kevin asked if we'd instead like to see the show from two folding chairs set up by the monitors just behind the stage. As soon as I sat, I saw on the monitor that the band had taken their spot and Ed McMahon was warming up the crowd on the microphone.

"You guys can sit here and enjoy the show, but try to stay quiet," said Kevin.

He then helped two attractive women in tight black dresses and hair sprayed magnificently into place take a seat next to us. The four of us were quiet as that familiar trumpet tune started the show and Carson came out for his monologue. After a break and a quick session of "Stump The Band," another break was taking place when a man came by us and hugged the two women. Turning to me, he held out his hand and said something charming in a deep British accent.

His name was Jeremy Irons, and he had won an Oscar for Best Actor recently for *Reversal of Fortune.* He's maybe better known as Scar in *The Lion King* or the bad guy, Simon

Gruber, opposite Bruce Willis's good guy John McClane in
Die Hard With a Vengeance.

I could only assume the two ladies were his girlfriends?
Wives? Wife and Housemaid? Mistress and Taxi Driver? I
don't know, Hollywood folks are weird, but they both
swooned over him when he left and said "he looks so good
out there!" to each other when he was on the couch next to
Johnny.

When the two ladies left, the next guest, a large man with a
glass of scotch in one hand and a cigar in the other was
introduced to me and my sister as comedian Louie
Anderson. In addition to a stand-up career and stint as host
of *Family Feud*, Anderson more recently has become known
as a three-time Emmy nominee for his work in the television
show *Baskets.*

He was still turned around talking to us when I heard Johnny
on the monitor say "ladies and gentlemen please help me
welcome our next guest, a very funny man, Mr. Louie
Anderson!"

The crowd began clapping but all Anderson could do was mutter an "aw shit" while he stubbed out the cigar and threw the glass down on a chair as he rushed over to the curtain for a delayed entrance.

After a third guest, some cowboy poet who had won zero Oscars or Emmys (lame!), the ending music started and I jumped out of my chair to head back towards the green room for some free Coke.

Before I could make it, however, a small entourage with flashing bulbs appeared like tourists in front of the Statue of Liberty. Johnny was coming through and all I could do was stand by. He waved off some of the photographers and didn't even notice me. It's like he knew I was a Letterman guy. A second later Ed came through. There were no photographers for him and he managed to wink at me the way you would do for someone who didn't receive a Publisher's Clearing House check. Having spent my life in someone's shadow playing the role of backup, I really felt Ed.

The Berenger friendship with my dad opened other avenues, as well. Tom may or may not have come into the funeral home on occasion to hang out. My sister may or may not have been a babysitter to his three kids.

I don't know if Tom had anything to do with Dad being discovered by the novelist Kathy Reichs, but she did base a minor character in one of her books on the Beaufort County Coroner. The book *Death Du Jour* is the second book in the series of books by Reichs that features main character Temperance Brennan. You might better know her now as the lead character in the television series *Bones*, based on the novels, where Brennan is portrayed by actress Emily Deschanel.

Reichs came to Beaufort for research about the novel that featured a plotline of cult activity in Beaufort. She spent several days with Dad observing and asking questions. Before the television series there was talk of a film adaptation of the novel, in which it was floated that the character based on my dad would be portrayed by actor Sam Elliot. This thrilled my mom to no end because she'd have easily traded my dad in for the real Sam Elliot. Beef was what she wanted for dinner, apparently.

Then again, maybe Reichs had just seen the famous episode of *Unsolved Mysteries* where Dad was interviewed about a missing persons case and had to recreate - along with several Beaufort County Sheriff's Deputies and EMS workers - several scenes in a lowcountry marsh. Indisputably, a man named Dan Tondevold had worked his way into the life of an elderly Tennessee widow named Ellen Berry. He'd become her chauffeur and who knows what else at her ancestral Tennessee mansion, Berrymount. Tondevold had worked his way so deep into Berry's life that she'd even given him power-of-attorney, so when he suggested a vacation to Charleston in late 1984, she'd happily gone along.

Here's where it gets weird.

Before leaving for Charleston by car, Tondevold had placed an ad in South Carolina newspapers seeking a chauffeur for use during their time there. Men who answered the ad also had to oddly submit a photograph.

By early 1985 they decided to go back to Tennessee, but Tondevold arranged for Berry to fly back while he would drive their Mercedes instead of them driving together the way they'd come.

Berry arrived back in Tennessee to find the power had been cut to her home and the bank was planning a foreclosure as she was suddenly and desperately out of funds.

Tondevold never made it back.

He'd instead gone to Fripp Island in Beaufort and ran up an enormous debt on Berry's credit, presumably what was left that he hadn't already spent. When he ran out, he wrote a suicide note and left his body to be found in the marshes of Fripp.

That's where my dad comes in.

When the body was found, nearby it was a gun belonging to Berry and a wallet with her credit cards. No identification was on him, however, and Dad called in security guards who had seen Tondevold on the island for the previous week to say "yeah, that's the guy."

It's a precarious way to identify the dead, but lacking more information and knowing that things in 1985 weren't exactly CSI-level, it seemed to work, especially when a handwritten suicide note was found in his room on Fripp. At least that's what Dad told the interviewers for *Unsolved Mysteries*.

There were and are rumors, naturally, that the man who washed up in the marsh wasn't Tondevold at all, but rather the chauffeur who was hired. Thinking that he'd be able to pass for a Tondevold lookalike, the rumor is that Tondevold shot this man and left him while he himself got away in the darkness.

Of course, no one ever filed a missing persons report on any chauffeur, and as Tondevold was supposedly a closeted gay man who had run out of his elderly friend's money, the suicide theory does seem to make more sense.

Still, Dad kind of put himself out there being on television discussing a truly mysterious case. He opened himself up to armchair detectives and others who didn't like him discussing the case so publicly.

"There is no reason for me to believe it was anyone but Dan Tondevold," said Dad. "I'm not going to say that that's not a possibility, but I certainly do not believe it to be one."

He was a minor celebrity for a while as *Unsolved Mysteries* was a popular show at the time. Reruns are still seen on Lifetime: Television for Women. I know this because I still get people who say they've seen it. They don't mind admitting that they watch Lifetime, I guess.

None of the reruns or even the first showing on a major television network (which we definitely taped on our state of the art VCR) were worth what happened in the reenactment. It took an entire afternoon to film police "finding" the body and Dad being called to the scene to "investigate." He came home scratching himself that night and I remember the image of my mom dabbing calamine lotion on the 200-plus chigger bites on his legs. I can't even imagine what the actor who played the corpse had to endure.

Anyway, having met celebrities and been on television shows and interviewed for books gave Dad a certain comfort with the limelight. There are those like me who would be mortified with the attention, but it just emboldened Dad.

During the height of his newfound chutzpah, at a celebrity sports auction on Hilton Head one night, my dad called me from his cell phone around 9:00pm. Thinking it must have surely been an emergency, I answered, only to hear Dad say "hang on, I've got someone here who wants to talk to you."

I waited a second and finally heard "Hey Ryan, it's Sid Bream here."

He might as well have said "It's Braves and Pirates legend Sid Bream here."

He went on to ask me how I was doing. At 9pm on a random night. I would like to think it was as awkward a conversation for him as it was for me, but he went on to give a mini-inspirational speech and quoted Bible verses to me. All I really wanted was to ask him what it was like to score the winning run in the '92 NLCS.

Dad came home with a signed bat that night, but in addition to the Sid Bream signature he had seriously devalued it by adding another verse of scripture. It wasn't like it was a game-used bat Jesus himself had stepped up to the plate with against Pontius Pilate.

Anyway, I always had fun picturing my dad going up to Bream like they were buddies.

"Hey Sid, come here!" he said. "Do me a favor and talk to my kid on the phone, would you? He loves baseball and all you light-hitting, defensive-minded first basemen!"

That's a joke, of course, but it can be said that while my dad loved his work, he definitely did not mind the celebrity that somehow ended up coming with it. It was an extension of his in-your-face personality that allowed fame to somehow find a small-town funeral director and coroner, even if he didn't always actively seek it.

He just kind of had a knack for getting in front of well-known people and not shrinking in the moment. He even gave me a shot in 1988 when he picked me up from school during the middle of the day to take me down to the Waterfront Park for a meet-and-greet with Vice President George Bush. You might remember him as George Bush I, George, Sr., George

H.W. Bush or simply "the one who could pronounce 'nuclear' correctly."

At that time Bush was currently in office as the nation's number two but running in a crowded primary for nomination to the top spot. He would win, of course, and he was already the front runner, but Dad knew that when a sitting veep and presumptive future president comes to your town you don't pass it up.

As the son of a history teacher, even I knew at that point that Beaufort had already been visited by George Washington, U.S. Grant, Franklin Roosevelt and Ronald Reagan. In the 2000's Mom and Dad went to a dinner party at the mayor's house for guest-of-honor and presidential candidate John McCain.

In 1988, though, it did not matter why we were going downtown in the middle of a school day, it just meant that I got out of math class. No more fractions today, buddy, I'm taking three fifths of the day to get outta this clown school!

Dad parked at the waterfront and we got out of his Crown Victoria to rush under the covered pavilion just as a light drizzle began, the gray of the sky momentarily reflected in the Beaufort River.

We were placed along the front row of the receiving line, which I suspect had something to do with Dad's involvement in Carroll Campbell's gubernatorial campaign in Beaufort County, as Campbell helped chair Bush's South Carolina election committee.

Before I knew it, the hundred or so of us crowded under the covered roof turned to see a vice-presidential limousine come spinning into the circular driveway next to the park. A man in a dark blue suit stepped out to the flash of camera bulbs.

I waited in line until Vice President Bush reached me, and as he stood in front of me I looked up to see a tall man with a granite face. He was smiling, but he looked Herculean from my vantage point. It was clear he was a Very Important Person who knew how to handle himself in public. He reached down and shook my hand, then knelt in front of me to sign an autograph for me, using a piece of paper I'd pulled from that dreaded math notebook just half an hour before.

For a moment, the flashbulbs stopped and the rain quieted and Vice President Bush looked me directly in the eye and said "I didn't even know Curt had a son!"

Kidding. He actually went on through the line and moved towards a microphone where I'm sure he said something about being prudent during the rest of the election season. I honestly can't remember, nor do I know what happened to my dad in the crowd because he definitely was no longer behind me. All I can say is that I vowed to never wash my hands again and from that point on I would follow the life and career of George H.W. Bush with an eagle eye. Personal encounters with greatness will do that to a normal person.

My vow to not wash my hands was not as great as my need to cleanse them of germs every fifteen minutes. Still, President Bush could have called me and asked me to skydive with him over Houston in 2014 and I would have done it.

When we left the park that day after finally having located Dad in the throng of reporters, I had an autograph from a future president and a notion that even school can be missed for some reasons that aren't always apparent to a third-grader.

One final anecdote from the files of the somewhat-famous includes Dad's encounters with the Conroy family. No book based in Beaufort is complete without some recognition of writer Pat Conroy and his impact on the town.

As recounted by Pat himself in "The Death of Santini," Dad had already had a strange encounter with Pat's sister at the funeral for their brother. Dad was verbally abused on the church steps by her over her being left out of being a pallbearer at her mother's funeral some years before, despite him having nothing to do with that sound decision.

Most everyone knew by then that Colonel Donald Conroy, aka The Great Santini himself, was a notorious brute in his younger years, ruling with an iron fist before age and fame softened him considerably. Dad buried Santini himself in 1998.

But what Pat's book about the death of his father didn't mention was that the night before the funeral, at the visitation for Pat's younger brother, as the crowd was filing out and the service winding down, Dad stood in the vestibule talking with Pat about a case in the national news where a mother had been found guilty of killing her own two children by drowning them in the bathtub in a fit of anger.

"I can't imagine any parent feeling that way about their own child!" my dad said offhandedly.

"Curt, can I introduce you to my father?" said Pat.

Colonel Conroy turned around, smirked at the joke and walked away quietly.

CHAPTER VIII.

Despite his protestation that funeral directors weren't "vultures" and many of them were "friendly people who just wanted to help others," none of his best friends were fellow funeral industry people.

Throughout his time in Beaufort, the people he was closest to were fellow Southern men who sought to put their energies and talents into making the community better. He chose friends with "regular" professions like furniture store owner and city manager and insurance salesman. His best friends were men like Ed Duryea, a tailor-shop owner on USMC Recruit Depot Parris Island, Gerry Hutchison, a DNR agent and Lowell Keene, whom he once hired to manage a travel agency.

What's that you say, a travel agency and a funeral home owner?! Too much business acumen rolled into one skinny individual?

You're right, it was too much, which is why nothing besides the funeral home ever really lasted long.

In addition to being coroner for 28 years, Dad had a multitude of other jobs to keep him busy. He also had my mom and her steady teaching job, which always allowed him a little security to take risks in the small business world.

The funeral home was what he held onto the longest and where his passion truly lay. However, in the time I knew him, he also owned a real estate company, two separate travel agencies, another funeral home in a different location, an ice cream shop, a florist shop and an arcade. If I'm missing something, forgive my memory. He owned a couple of them simultaneously but not all of them at once.

I don't remember the real estate company too well, but it was called Lowcountry Realty and has gone on to do well after he sold his interest. The travel agency was the first that I remember going into and knowing it was (partially?) mine.

Set up in an old bank, the agents were situated behind a walk up desk where the bank tellers used to be. You know, when you're trying to book a Jamaican cruise you might as well feel as if you're handing your money over to a stolid institution.

Hanging from the ceiling were paper and plastic miniatures of airplanes, cruise ships and railroad cars. The chairs set up for folks to sit privately with an agent to discuss that holiday road vacation to Des Moines were covered in green and orange felt. The place smelled, as all businesses Dad owned, like coffee that had been sitting in the pot long enough to have molded.

While I struck out, personally, with interest in the real estate or travel agencies, I didn't mind the news that came home one night that Dad had bought an ice cream shop and arcade. I was an early teenager then, and Bay Cafe and Ice Cream and Bay Arcade, situated next to each other in the Old Bay Marketplace (also on Bay Street, also across from an actual bay) was soon to become my favorite hangout.

Surrounded by mom and pop shops that sold art and books and knick-knacks, the ice cream shop and arcade served as a perfect metaphor for my dad. They were accepted by their peers even if they stood out just a little from the rest.

He would later call it his "ice cream mistake," as if he'd gotten a sugar cone full of rocky road when he'd meant to get a cup of strawberry. What he didn't get in the business deal was lots of income. Even though neither the cafe nor the arcade lasted, they both gave me a good reason to be downtown on Saturdays.

He had managers for both places, of course, but as the owner's son I was expected to work for free behind the counter at the ice cream and sandwich shop and only play in the arcade if there wasn't a line for the games.

I was never much of a gamer, but NBA Jamz was my jam. Getting to play two-on-two basketball as the Charles Barkley and Dan Majerle-led Phoenix Suns against the Bill Laimbeer and Isiah Thomas-led Pistons? Yeah, a kid could get lost in the dark for hours there.

Unfortunately, there was always a ham to slice or a coffee cup to refill or another ice cream sundae (with fresh bananas!) to fix. Was it against child labor laws for me to technically work there? Yes. Did I mind that the place was chock full of older teen girls who were suddenly "coworkers" of mine? Not at all.

Plus, the place attracted some strange regular clientele.

In addition to the jeweler down the way who would lock his shop to come in for a cup of coffee and the occasional sandwich, I noticed we had an older couple who came in nearly every day in the late afternoon at around the same time for a bowl of ice cream and a cup of coffee while sitting in the same chairs at the same table.

Sometimes they would bring their dogs with them and feed them ice cream from the same spoon, which endeared them to some but grossed me out to the point that I refused to pick up the spoons after they left. They were retired and lived downtown, so it made sense that they would walk and have their daily outing in the ice cream shop.

The wife, Aileen, had strawberry blonde hair and often wore matching sweatshirts and sweatpants. Even in the heat of August. She'd been a nurse in the Great War and loved to talk about all the soldiers she'd tended to on the battlefield. Her husband, Felix, was a retired civil service worker who almost never spoke but would sometimes stutter a "that's right dear" when Aileen was recounting a story.

Felix was always smiling, even on the afternoon that it was raining and he pulled into a spot right outside the cafe in his car, which he got out of to check all four doors to ensure that they were locked. Today we'd call that obsessive-compulsive disorder. Back then I wrote it off to the eccentric charm of small-town folks.

They even celebrated my 14th birthday with me, albeit arbitrarily. They were there in their usual spots when I came in genuinely surprised by the setup my friends had planned.

I was supposed to be going to the movies with one of the older girls who worked at the cafe, Julie. I may have walked around in the days leading up to the "date" letting everyone know what a big deal I had become. Julie was intelligent, attractive and incredibly kind. We'd hung out at the cafe (well, she was legitimately working and I was goofing off) and played tennis together on occasion, like a married couple on Fripp Island whose pace was matched by their age. The idea of going to the movies with her, however, was unfathomable. I'd have watched a complete French mime show just for the chance to be around her.

On the way to the movies, however, she turned the car around to retrieve the wallet she'd "left" at the cafe. I walked in with her to find a birthday cake surrounded by my friends

Katy, Daniel, Meredith, Felix, Aileen and others. I loved them all dearly, but I think the disappointment on my face at not going to the movies with Julie was apparent to all.

The cafe and arcade were closed not long after that, though we kept the signs from both places in my parents' garage. The old demon Unprofitability reared its head again in one of Dad's ancillary businesses. The signage and the memory of a sandwich that was briefly named for me (The Ryan!) is all I have now.

If you're wondering, it was a corned beef on white with mustard and bacon. According to daily receipts it was ordered zero times in two years.

I didn't have much more luck years later with my dad's florist shop. It was smart, really, that he bought a florist shop with the idea that "people buy arrangements for funerals a lot anyway so I might as well double-dip." It just didn't work out as planned.

For one, he caught at least two employees embezzling from him, which is the same thing that happened when he had the travel agency. And a part time employee from the funeral home was once caught with money from the business literally in the trunk. You might say it was an issue.

His management style, to the degree he ever formalized one, was to hire people who didn't need much oversight. As referenced above, that sometimes backfired, but in general he was stretched into so many directions there was no possible way to stay on top of every person's actions who could claim they worked for a facet of Copeland Company, the LLC he formed to be the umbrella over all his ventures.

Another thing he formed with intent was a document called "ccdead." We found copies of it after his death. There were versions that had been edited over the years and changed with various word processors according to the software available, but it was essentially a directive for what to do with his holdings after his death. His own father had died young, so he had a certain fatalistic belief that he would not reach old age himself.

The document was somewhat laughable in the fact that it was far outdated and not legally enforceable. It listed businesses he no longer even owned at his actual death along with descriptions of certain employees who were "capable" or "trustworthy" to take over in his absence. Ed

Duryea, of course, was listed as the person most responsible for assuming a "chairman of the board" type position over all assets. The document, however, even listed the hymns that were to be played at Dad's funeral and in which key by which organist.

I really did look for a sentence that said "continue to deny Ryan's existence, hereafter referred to as 'the boy,' but give Shelley most if not all of any existing inheritance, unless Judy intervenes on behalf of the boy."

I didn't find it, of course, but it was clear he took his jobs and his imagined empire seriously. He had built everything he had himself and really from the ground floor of his elemental upbringing in Greer. Of course he wanted things to go on after he was gone. Someone should inherit that entrepreneurial spirit, even if he couldn't look on at it from above, and even if the attorney who was hired to enact these plans had long passed, himself.

Though at the time of the document's writing my sister was fifteen and I was 9, Dad really did write "as of this date I would like to keep everything intact until the children have the opportunity to be part of the business. That is going to be difficult if not impossible. Although neither child has expressed any interest in following in the business, when they get older they may see opportunities. I must admit that Shelley does like money. Ryan, unfortunately, seems to be too much like me and money is not the most important thing around."

It still isn't for me, so he was right about that, but he was also being modest about what he made and what fun he had trying out different avenues of small business.

His dream customer would have been someone who woke up in the morning and headed to Bay Cafe for coffee, stopping only to play a couple of rounds of Mrs. Pac Man at the arcade next door. After breakfast this person would head to the florist to get a bouquet of roses to take by the travel agency and thank the agent who helped them book that dream vacation to Decatur last month. They would inform the agent that they loved Decatur so much they were moving there and putting their house up for sale with Lowcountry Realty. After leaving the travel agency the person would of course take a wrong turn into traffic and run into a light pole. Dad would be called to the scene to investigate and rule it "death by misadventure." In the dead person's wallet would be a card with a little note - "bury me with Copeland Funeral Home."

Personally, I suppose I could have turned down the keys to the funeral home in lieu of any of those other businesses. I could be writing this from the comfort of being surrounded by a thousand daisies and petunias and whatever the hell else you have in a florist shop. I didn't pay that much attention.

But I saw a man always taking risks and mostly losing money. It's honestly the American Way and I'm proud that he put so much effort into diversifying his funds and trying to make the community better at the same time. There's no charity or civic club he and his various enterprises didn't support financially.

Still, that lifestyle wasn't for me. That American Way hadn't been inherited by me.

I must be, secretly, Czechoslovakian.

CHAPTER IX.

I first met Leigh Priester sometime in the church nursery, I assume. Born just three months after me, our parents attended the same church. Since we lived just a few blocks from each other growing up, we also ended up attending the same elementary school, middle school and high school together.

It wasn't until I was a student at Clemson University and she was a student at rival University of South Carolina that she deemed me acceptable to date - albeit from a safe two-hour distance. If you can make it through that as a couple, you can make it through anything.

As those things go, we were married in 2003 even while I was still finishing up my last semester of coursework. Yes, she finished on time in 2002, but Clemson is much more rigorous. I am also much less intelligent than she.

Her mother was a librarian and her father was a postal service worker, both of them quiet and unassuming. I think my dad's personality and habit of having dinner table discussions on any topic intimidated her at first, even if she'd known him almost as long as I had.

I do think she genuinely thought she was marrying into a family with a situation where either I or my sister would eventually take over Dad's businesses. She knew I didn't go to college necessarily to study current embalming procedures, but she did know it was there as a "fallback" and that my dad did still want me to do something under the Copeland Company umbrella.

Suffice it to say that I was no self-made man. Even if I rejected the funeral business, I first worked for a small magazine in a job my dad found for me. I parlayed that into a much higher-paying job working sales in a medical company that also advertised in the magazine. I was terrible at that and any subsequent sales job, but no matter where I went I was known as Curt's son. Let's take an introvert who doesn't like talking to people and make him talk to people who already know who he is because of his last name. It would have been easier to just work for him directly.

I ended up doing some work for him anyway, just like old times but without the tractor or the warm cremated remains in the passenger seat.

He called me up at that awful sales job one day and asked if I wanted to meet him for lunch at Applebee's. I suggested fast food but you can't kill a classy idea like Applebee's.

We were probably just finishing up those awesome microwaved mozzarella sticks when Dad got a call on his cell phone. When he finished the conversation he turned to me. I knew what was coming because I'm no dummy. I've seen The Godfather, Part III. Just when you think you're out…

"Can you come help me with something?" he asked.

I had no choice. He'd picked me up for lunch so I was at his mercy.

He left me to pay the bill while he ran back to the funeral home to get the hearse. When he came back into the parking lot to get me I looked both ways and sprinted towards the passenger door, hoping no one would see me get in.

As we headed back into traffic, Dad reached again for his cell phone and called his office back.

"Who is it again?" I heard him say.

I couldn't hear the other end of the conversation but I heard him hang up and whisper to himself a couple of times. The word he said was "rice," so I thought maybe he'd forgotten to order it at lunch or maybe he just loved it so much he had developed a ritual of whispering it to himself.

He turned off the main road in Beaufort and headed down into the Hermitage area, the neighborhood where my grandparents lived. He took a right at the end and pulled left into a long driveway that ended with a small white house on the banks of Battery Creek.

We were at the home of the daughter of Carew Rice, Jr. The elderly Rice had just passed away maybe an hour before. Though he was a respected engineer himself, it was his father, Carew, Sr., who was known all over South Carolina for his unique artistry in using construction paper to cut silhouette portraits, something Clay Rice (Carew Sr.'s grandson) carries on today.

Dad had thoughtfully brought the stretcher with him, and as we walked into the room overlooking the water where he was still lying in a hospital bed, I noticed how quiet it was. You could almost hear the tide coming in against the bare oyster beds.

His daughter finally broke the silence.

"I was just sitting next to him reading a book of recipes aloud," she said. "I think it was the spinach casserole that put him over."

I stifled a laugh because she'd delivered it deadpan.

My dad did not think it was a joke, however, and looked at me to tell me to lift Mr. Rice's feet onto the stretcher at the same time he would move the upper body.

Even though he was likely still warm, I did not want to touch his legs. Dead skin and all. I decided an alternative method would be to grab the sheets around his legs and use them to move him. It was nothing personal, it was just that he was dead and I was not and human nature is to always be cautious around things that are different.

We successfully got him onto the stretcher but had to awkwardly maneuver the stretcher around in the hallway so we could get him out of the house feet-first. It has something to do with keeping the head above the torso when coming down steps.

We got him in the hearse and I eventually got back to work, where any other employer would have fired me for taking an unannounced two hour lunch break. Of course, after I told them I was with my dad they shrugged it off, because going on death calls during lunch is normal for a medical salesperson.

Regardless, I had done well enough that a few nights later I got a call late in the night from my dad asking me to assist him again. I told Leigh I'd be back soon and went to the closet to get dressed.

"Do you even want to go?" she asked.

"Not really, but what am I going to say?"

I had to change out of my regular comfort wear - khaki shorts and a t-shirt from the Reagan era - and into something more acceptable. Dad always said you had to be presentable and professional when you were taking someone from their place of death in full view of those who loved them.

At the time I lived on Lady's Island and had to drive just a very short distance in my own neighborhood to get to the house. In fact, I beat my dad there, so I waited in the truck by myself in hopes that no one would look out the window and report an awkwardly suspicious white dude looking like the grim reaper.

Dad finally arrived and we went into a nice, older brick house with a meticulously manicured lawn. We were led to a small, dimly lit room off of a hallway and saw a very elderly man in a hospital bed with a hospice nurse beside him.

"It was about forty-five minutes ago," she said.

"Thank you, we can get it from here if you want to wait outside with his family," Dad told her.

I watched as he carefully, and I mean slowly and carefully, detached all the tubes and devices running from the man's nose and arms and legs and wrapped them on the side of the bed. When that was done, the man looked a little more fully human and less like a cyborg.

His mouth was wide open, but Dad only covered his entire body with a sheet that we then grabbed and used to shift him onto the stretcher. Relaxing his jaw enough to shut it would require some massaging and manipulation. It obviously wasn't the time and place for that.

When we'd loaded the body into the back of the hearse and shut the door, Dad only had two things to say.

"Next time, maybe wear a coat," he said.

Then he looked at me, gave pause, and asked if I'd be able to help him again from time to time, since Lady's Island was now "my area."

Of course, that was just a geographic area. I still struggled to reconcile my feelings for a business that made a lot of money but also took a lot of time. I wasn't prepared to drop everything I had - which now included a wife, full-time job and would soon be adding a child - for something I knew would require me to be on-call at all hours and physically present for the grieving process of people I'd be both on intimate terms with and completely unfamiliar.

That's probably what the public doesn't understand about a funeral business. When a financial adviser gets home from work he may or may not kick off his shoes and turn it to CNBC. After the stock market closes, he may think about the next day's exchange but he more than likely pours a stiff drink, rubs his son's head and kisses his wife on the cheek before he heads back out to the backyard to practice his golf swing.

The funeral business never stops.

Dad would leave work and call the answering service to begin their hours. They would take calls and forward the most urgent ones directly to my dad.

If he did get a call and had to go get a body at an inconvenient hour he'd have to get it back to the funeral home and decide when he had to prepare it. If there were pre-arrangements made for the service he'd have a better idea, but he'd have to have the family of the deceased in his office the next day to talk over details of the service and the burial.

He'd have to listen to their stories about their loved ones, give them time to compose themselves, sell them a casket, talk to them about fees (when they'd almost rather do anything but), discuss burial clothes, coordinate with churches and ministers and pallbearers, talk about gravesite and headstones, all within a 24-48 hour span. And that's just if there is one death per day, which of course doesn't always happen.

Not only did he have to see people at their lowest, they had to deal with him in a situation slightly less pleasant than meeting with an IRS agent in person. He was acutely aware that he was not high on the list of people anyone really wanted to see, so he tried to keep things in his office - pictures of his kids and grandkids, a saxophone-playing plastic M&M, a desktop water fountain - to remind the grieving family that they, too, were dealing with a human who had experienced the death of a loved one.

Not all that I did involved meeting him at a house to pick up someone whose blood was no longer circulating.

My mom called me one night to see if I could run out to the funeral home and check on my dad. He hadn't been home since the early afternoon and it was now nearly 10pm.

What I found when I got there was that the light was only on in the garage where the crematory was. Dad - with considerable help from several other people - had put a 600lb man in around midday. It would be close to midnight before it was over.

Here's a little hint about a crematory - if you pass a funeral home during the day and see smoke coming from behind a building somewhere, it ain't charbroiled burgers back there. It's why Dad preferred to have it run at night.

This night he was afraid to leave it because of the time it had been in use and the size of the body using it.

"How long do you think this is going to be?" I asked him when I entered.

"About another two hours, I guess," he said as he sighed.

"Mom's worried about you," I told him.

"She sent you out here?" he asked before turning away. "I told her it would be a while. Why don't you go on home?" he asked.

"I just got here."

"You don't have to stay out here though. I know you don't like it."

He said it as if normal people walked around saying "you know, my life is missing a certain element where I get to spend time around the cremation process!"

Still, kudos to him for realizing I wasn't cut out for it.

I told him I'd go but asked if he needed anything - a cup of coffee or anything like that - because he was just standing there in an empty garage with a single panel light waiting for the red light of the furnace to turn off.

"No, I'm good," he said. "It's better than yesterday."

"What happened yesterday?" I asked, my curiosity genuinely piqued.

"A boy your age committed suicide and I had to put him in there, but before I did his mother wanted to see him one last time."

"I know him," I said. "I knew him, anyway."

Andrew, the boy my age, had gone to high school with me. He was quiet, dressed in dark clothes and was a seriously skilled musician. He never talked much and didn't seem to have too many friends. He was an outcast, but the kind that was friendly and seemed to enjoy being different. He never struck me as angry. If anything he was too peaceful and mature for other high school kids with raging hormones and angst. I didn't know what caused him to end all that, but I hoped it wasn't because he felt like he didn't have a place.

"Well, because of what he did there wasn't anything I could do but put a few towels and sheets over most of him and leave his arms out," he said. "His mother wanted to hold his hand one more time, so I waited and watched as she held his hand, talked to him, buried her own head on his arm..."

He trailed off.

When I looked I saw that he no longer even realized I was still in the room. He was probably back to that moment the day before. Maybe now even to a similar moment with a similar mom and son from some other instance. It was hard to tell, sometimes, because he'd seen and dealt with so much.

I left him that night to deal with his own demons, but soon got another chance for another body pickup about a month later when I got a late afternoon call from my dad to join him in the parking lot at Sherwin Williams on Lady's Island.

"Someone died at Sherwin Williams?" I asked.

"No, son, just meet me there," he said.

"Are you picking out paint?"

"No! I need your help getting a body from the island."

"Well I can drive to wherever you need."

"Not to this place."

"Well just give me the address and I can plug it into GPS," I said.

"Meet me at the paint store," he said, and I could feel his exasperation reach through the line like that Freddy Krueger movie where Freddy's tongue comes through the phone and licks the woman's ear.

When he got to the store I jumped in the passenger seat and our routine continued in person.

"Where am I going?" he asked.

"I'm not sure, you didn't say," I said.

"I wasn't asking you, I was asking myself."

"Oh, sorry."

"Eddings Point Road," he said aloud as he read from a small piece of paper.

"Where is Eddings Point Road?" I asked.

"It's...it's out there."

We headed out onto Highway 21 towards St. Helena and as the airport came into view on our left Dad reached for the paper again.

He set it back down long enough for us to get to Dataw before he picked it up again.

The sun was setting already and starting to cower behind the tall pine trees that dotted the narrow roads that led to the beach. The glinting contrast would have stung my eyes had it not been for the tint of the window.

As we passed the country store on St. Helena, Dad said "where are we going again?" and I knew better than to answer. He looked at the paper once more and put it back down.

It was clear that his short-term memory was fading fast.

We finally, and to this day don't know how, reached a road with a turnoff onto a one-way dirt path that wound around more palms and pines and up to a house on the water. To this day I couldn't get back if I tried.

Dad got out of the car, saw a middle-aged woman standing at the top of the front porch, and adjusted himself by buttoning his coat button and taking his reading glasses back off.

I looked at the stairs, steeper and more numerous than even old Wayman Price's, and thought "this shit's going to be fun. I'm gonna drop this guy for sure!"

When Dad reached the top of the stairs the woman broke down and hugged my dad. I wasn't prepared for either of those emotional reactions.

When she'd composed herself she said "I'm sorry...I'm just not okay."

All Dad said was "you're not supposed to be."

We walked into the back of the house towards the bedroom. When we got into the spacious bedroom with the view of the water, I noticed how different things were from the last call I'd gone on. Unlike the elderly man in my neighborhood, this was clearly a man taken before his time. Lying in his own bed instead of a hospital-provided bed, the man had only small flecks of gray on his full head of hair. Instead of his mouth it was his eyes that were open this time.

Again, that could be adjusted later.

"Those are just his pajamas," his wife said. "Does he need more clothes?"

"No," Dad replied. "This is fine. We can take care of that later."

"When do I come in to talk about a service?" she asked as we moved the body onto the stretcher.

"You come anytime that's convenient for you. Do you want to say 10:00 in the morning?" he asked her.

"Well, I doubt I'll get much sleep tonight," she said.

"Want to make it 8AM?"

"Yes, that would be better."

He had a knack for understanding when people needed to tend to things like funeral arrangements. He always made himself available to their timeframe and not vice versa. It's like he knew she was apprehensive about what the next steps were, so taking that worry from her by giving her the option of taking care of it first thing in the morning probably helped.

Before we left, he went back to her on the porch for one more question.

"Do you have someone to stay the night with you, some friends or someone?"

"My daughter is on her way in from Atlanta," she said. "She should be here before 11."

I think experience had maybe taught him that people in her situation shouldn't be alone. Either that or his basic decency kicked in yet again, the way it had when we'd first shown up.

On the way back into town, I had to remind him to drop me back off to get my truck at Sherwin Williams.

In private, his memory was increasingly failing. It was mostly short-term lapses, the kind where you can't remember what you had for breakfast but were fine when it came to remembering that Swingin' Medallions concert in 1967.

His forgetfulness unfortunately coincided with the rise of internet message boards and comment sections of online news outlets, even if social media was still a year or two away from catching on. I'd already discovered how mean people can be online, but I wasn't prepared for a post that caught my attention one night on the Beaufort Gazette website.

"What is our coroner doing??" was the topic of the post.

An anonymous person who alluded to having worked for EMS went to the front page of the Gazette online to post a litany of mistakes he felt Dad had made during his entire career as coroner. It was a thinly veiled attack on Dad's apparent battle with dementia. It wasn't public knowledge and it wasn't even diagnosed, but time spent around Dad gave you the impression at least something was slightly off.

That told me this anonymous poster knew my dad, and I eventually tracked down the person making the attacks, though I've kept the knowledge to myself to this day. I internalized the complaints anyway. There wasn't much point in making someone else who cared about him be just as miserable. Public officials are easy to criticize and sometimes legitimately so, but all of them also have families out there who like the person behind the job.

Other posters came to Dad's defense while some joined in the attack. Some of it was personal, others were raising questions that weren't necessarily bad to be raising.

I ended up staying up night after night for months when the Gazette's page would "update" with new stories and posts just to monitor the things said and the stories that were run in hopes none of them would involve my dad. It was the only time in being his son that I hated the effect what he did for a living had on me. I understood clearly why my mom had been against him running for sheriff in 1992 when some organizers had asked him to.

Probably no one was more relieved than me when his term and tenure as coroner finally ended in 2008 and his longtime deputy Ed Allen was elected. Ed has proven more than capable and just as empathetic in his own right, and the county was lucky he stepped up to run for an office that gets little in the way of public thanks.

When I helped my parents negotiate and sign the deal that sold both the funeral home and the cemetery to a family friend and businessman, I thought it was all over and Dad could maybe find some way to relax in his current state.

He'd have less than two years to live.

CHAPTER X.

Most of the time I had bonding with my dad, however little our different personalities made it over the years, revolved around food. He took me to two movies - just the two of us - when I was growing up, both after an early dinner at Broad River Seafood. He'd talk more to the waitresses and managers than he would me, but I didn't blame him. We didn't have much to say and I certainly wasn't going to talk to the people who worked at the restaurant. I was there to eat, they were there to bring me something to eat, and that was basically the end of the transaction. Nothing more needed to take place, except for my dad, who would talk to the animatronic animals at Chuck E. Cheese if afforded the chance.

After hearty meals of shrimp and hush puppies, we went to see the immortal *Ernest Goes to Jail*. Who said being a funeral director meant you didn't have time to enjoy classic movies with your son?! The theater was full of people who, like us, did not laugh once.

A year later we repeated the unenjoyable experience with a viewing of *Days of Thunder*. For once we could agree that neither of us liked NASCAR. So, of course, we cemented that bond by going to see a movie about NASCAR.

I think it was easier for him to have outings with me where we could at least eat and both take an active part in something. When I was in little league, before games he would take me to breakfast at Huddle House. Again, the place was full of "regulars" that he would spend time in conversation with while I'd load up on waffles and chocolate milk. Later, on the ballfield, once the nerves began to light themselves in my body, I'd throw it all back up before taking up my position at first base.

Aside from Huddle House, though, he was almost always after a classy meal. Anytime he wanted to take me somewhere to eat he'd insist on me choosing somewhere nice.

"What is it you want?" he'd ask.

"Burger King," I'd say.

"We're not going to Burger King! This is a nice day, we're going to go somewhere and sit down and have a nice meal," he'd reply.

I thought those smooth plastic benches at Burger King surrounded by sepia photos of *Gone With The Wind* were extremely classy.

One time we compromised and went to Hardees. He was so upset that we'd ended up at Hardees instead of having filleted fish and lamb chops at Whitehall Plantation on Lady's Island that he refused to get me a milkshake. Just on principle. The milkshake was the only reason I'd chosen Hardees.

As an adult my tastes hadn't changed much, but when he invited me to join his Rotary club I think it was less about the food and more about the company, at least by then. I was married now, permanently settled back in Beaufort and me joining his club was a way for him to keep tabs on me at least once a week. He had been the club's first president after its founding and was proud of the work the club had done in the community. Rotary was a club that, for him, allowed him to organize and participate in civic activities and converse with the movers and shakers in the small community.

Before I had joined officially I had already helped him drive around after the 2004 election and pick up political signs from yards in the neighborhood. We had to do it at night in case someone really, really wanted to keep that "Kerry/Edwards '04" banner for the garage. Believe it or not people were upset that the signs were taken down by the next morning, after their need had technically expired.

It was in that van-Dad driving and me doing the stealthy pick up work-that he first admitted he was slipping.

"I can't remember things like I used to," he said.

"I read a report in the New England Journal of Medicine that inhaling formaldehyde helped break up plaque on the brain," I said, trying my best to be scientifically helpful.

"Oh lord," he said. "I need all of that I can get. Your mother didn't even want me to run again for coroner this time."

In retrospect she might have been right. She usually was.

"Ah...you'll be alright," I told him.

That was my standard answer for not knowing the right answer. It also substituted for "mom is probably right."

"If you're helping with this you should really just come join Rotary," he said.

I told him I'd think about it and it only took me two years to accept. It was an acceptance of sorts into his social club, an acknowledgement that I, despite not being a funeral director or deputy coroner myself, was still a Copeland at heart and could do things for the community despite a lowly position.

We met weekly on Tuesdays, first in the dining room of the Holiday Inn and later in the old sanctuary-turned-fellowship hall of St. Peter's Catholic Church. It was there on a Tuesday in October of 2010 that I saw Dad start to cough. It wasn't unusual for a smoker of his ilk to have to clear his throat. Only this time, he took a drink of tea and continued to cough uncontrollably.

Sometimes at the meetings I sat with him, but more often than not I still tried to be my own person by casually sitting a table or two away, as if I were someone apart from just "Curt's son." I was sitting one table away when he started coughing, watching the whole thing. It's not a bonding experience at that point, but I still thought I'd leave him his dignity and not follow him outside as he left to catch his breath.

He came back in after the fit, but I called my mom later that night after I'd gotten home.

"Mom, Dad had a cough today that wouldn't go away," I told her matter-of-factly. "I think a doctor needs to look at him."

"Well, he has a physical scheduled for November," she said.

"I think we need to see if that can be moved up," I told her.

By the time he went to the doctor the next week, scans of his body showed a cancer that had already spread from his lungs into his colon, liver and brain. How long had he suffered physical discomfort without complaining.

"We can try treatment," his doctor told us. "It might only prolong the inevitable but would give you more time."

He left the room for my mom, my sister and me to think about it. There was nothing to discuss.

We hastily made arrangements for him to begin at-home hospice care and the prescribing of medicines that would ease pain, not kill errant cells. We went home, each of us, and began to have conversations with the larger, extended family about what would happen in the ensuing weeks. It was already early November and my niece, who was turning seven in a month, said "I hope G-Daddy makes it to my birthday."

As sweet as the sentiment was - a grandchild wanting her granddad to be part of just one more birthday celebration - for his sake I hoped he wasn't going to make it. That would only prolong the pain.

And it was painful.

I was over at my mom and dad's house one day in the back bedroom with Dad, where a hospital bed had been set up next to my parents' bed. He was literally moaning in his sleep with pain, and when he absentmindedly grabbed at his side I went over to him and lifted his shirt. The entire right side of his body was bruised. It was all internal, as the organs in him were so riddled with tumors that they had nowhere to go but outwards toward the skin. I put his shirt back down and let him continue trying to sleep.

I was over there again a couple of days later when I heard a thud. I was in the kitchen but knew the sound of something hitting the carpeted bedroom floor. When I got back there, Dad was lying next to the bed.

"I had to go to the bathroom," he said meekly.

I scooped him up, all 6'4 of him, and placed him back on the edge of the bed. He was so tired that his head drooped onto me. I carefully placed it back on his pillow and swung his legs back on the bed.

Yet, despite the physical toll the dying process was taking, something else amazing happened. His brain, so long dormant and less useful came back to life.

One night, as my mom cooked pork chops for everyone and I gathered with my wife, my son, my sister and her family,

Dad suddenly appeared at the dinner table. His seat had been left empty - I guess out of respect - but when he walked in it was a shock. He was more gaunt standing than he'd been sitting, but we didn't know he was capable of walking anymore, much less eating.

My mom said "Curt, do you really want to eat something?"

"It's dinnertime, isn't it?" he said.

As the weeks went on - and there were very few of them - word got out that if people in the community wanted to see him one last time they'd better come.

His friends from church, his friends from work, even neighborhood surgeons came by to visit. Some were people he might have forgotten about, but he stunningly recognized each of them and held genuine conversations with some. His recall and command of verbiage, so lacking in recent years, was suddenly clear.

I was sitting with him one Wednesday night because my mom had gone to church and didn't want him to be alone. He was in his hospital bed dozing while I was on a couch in their bedroom quietly studying for one of my graduate courses. When I heard him stir, I turned towards him.

"You need anything, Dad?" I asked.

"What did you call me?" he said.

"...Dad?"

"Oh, whew! I thought you called me 'Jeff!'"

Jeff was my brother-in-law.

He then asked me if my mom had gone to choir practice at church. He was making jokes, oriented to time and date...I had no explanation for it. If I were a researcher studying a link between cancer cells in your brain and dementia plaque, I could probably make something of it.

As it was, we were happy to have some semblance of him back before we had to say goodbye. That day came soon enough.

His neighbors, Ed and Cindy Duryea, were among the last to see him, as was their daughter Katy, visiting from Nashville and long ago forgiven for driving the car into the garage. Ed had come over the night before Dad passed and had to leave the room in tears and frustration, not yet ready for the moment. Cindy, however, sat by Dad's bedside and told him it was okay to go, something people in the act of dying legitimately have to hear, consciously or subconsciously, before their body gives them permission to shut down.

When my mom called me the next morning to tell me he hadn't taken a breath in over five minutes, I wasn't entirely surprised. I got dressed and headed over and made a pot of coffee in my mom's kitchen.

It was easy to stay calm. I'd seen my dad in this role hundreds of times. Now it was my turn to be on that end. I took a phone call from the media and then, as they took his body out of the house he built on a stretcher with a blanket that still had his name on it, I hugged my sister for the first time in years.

I'm not demonstrative, but even I know when someone needs comfort. I had a good role model for that.

Only a couple of days later I spoke at his funeral. The night before the funeral we had gathered at the funeral home still bearing his name to greet the outpouring of community members who stopped by. It was an open casket, but I noticed, before the line that eventually snaked outside and into the street formed, that dad's hair was parted the wrong way. I quickly asked the staff for a comb and fixed it myself. It was one of those tiny details that I'm surprised I noticed, but I know he would have been proud of me catching something that minute. It was odd being in that building for his own visitation, but the staff was wonderful and to this day anyone who uses the funeral home that still bears his name is considered family by all of us.

After everyone had left my mom told me and my sister, along with our spouses Leigh and Jeff, it was "time to say goodbye to your father." I didn't make my goodbyes long and wordy because I had to get back home to actually type out the eulogy for the next day. I'd already given the eulogy at my grandmother's funeral the year before and would give another at my great aunt's two years later. Oddly, it felt...natural. Speaking publicly about the death of a loved one intimidated me not one bit, even if it took doing it once to realize it. I'm also available for hire as a professional eulogizer if you want to take note.

But as I spoke about him from the pulpit that day, I realized part of his legacy in the funeral business would end with us. My sister took embalming classes at one point because she had interest in joining the family business. Together, with her handling the scientific aspect and me handling the grief process and service details, it might have worked. As we're both teachers, however, just like Mom before us, it looks as though the family business is, in actuality, education.

Having two sons of my own now I can tell you every father wants to have children in their own image. There's a biblical allusion there, sure, but also an innate human desire to pass on to the next generation the skills and biological tendencies that you, yourself, possess. Dad was no different. If I owned a bookshop or a haberdashery, I'd probably want it to be "Copeland and Son" someday, too.

Truthfully, the pressure to be in the business was all on me. Certainly he brought me along to so many of his calls and work-related functions and had me do increasingly responsible jobs at the funeral home because he thought I might find something I could hook into, but it takes the special set of skills that very few, ultimately including me, possess.

I have sympathy for grieving families and still there are people who come to me for advice on how to deal with grief in the loss of a loved one, but that's the extent of my abilities. I have next to no interest in learning to embalm, though I've seen it done a few times. I have even less interest in sitting in a quiet room trying to get the lifelike makeup right on someone whose soul has long departed. However, all of those pale in comparison to the need to be home.

Dad did his best to keep some semblance of balance. His work called to him in the waking hours as often as it did those of cloud-covered nights. The man was asleep by 9pm every night on his couch, if he slept at all. Yet he never missed my baseball games - even the away games. His mind might have been on getting Mrs. Morgan's death certificate completed or preparing a statement for a council meeting or just ensuring coverage for whatever employee was on vacation that week, but he was physically there. He was accessible, even if there wasn't much for us to confer about in our overlapping free hours.

Having shared some tendencies, I realize now that he was just restless. He was never so much in the moment as already moving on to the next.

Still, after his death people I didn't know felt compelled to come up to me and tell me the nice things he did for them. He bought Christmas toys for a gas station clerk's children. He heavily discounted funeral costs for people down on their luck. He wrote letters in support of people or against some cause that others deemed offensive. He was generally in the corner of the "little guy" even when in the dining room party of the "big guy." I learned more about him from others after his death than I ever did during his life.

And I couldn't think of anything aside from the times when I got sick and he stayed up all night with me washing my face with a washcloth and watching midnight reruns of *Magnum, Pl.* Or the times he came over and helped me build a raised garden bed or install chair rail in my son's bedroom, working silently by my side. How he'd laugh harder at my jokes than anyone else. That's all I could think about.

He never saw me turn into a fully-functioning adult with a job and wife and two kids. He was gone by the time I was 30, but I'd dealt without his counsel for far longer than that. Most of what I've tried to do so far in my life has been so far out of the shadow now cast by his gravestone that I'm not sure he'd recognize me. I identify with the restlessness.

As my friend Justin Hardy mentioned in an earlier interview, death being a part of life was ironic. Perhaps an even greater irony for me is that as I struggle identifying with my older son, Lukas, I realize it's because he's just like my dad. My younger son, Reames, is much more "conventional" and easygoing. Raising Lukas is like raising my dad, but I have nothing to leave him as a legacy.

I own no businesses myself, as Lukas is quick to point out. I can pass along my love of books and learning, but that's something very common among the populace already. When he was younger, Lukas started his own "Copeland Industries" fundraising organization that included a website, business cards and posters. He went around the neighborhood soliciting funds that he could then turn in to the United Way. It was all very above-the-board but I was still mortified. It was so...unlike me.

I should also mention that he was about 8 or 9 at the time.

In addition to his own business plan, he created and ordered business cards for me, despite the fact that somehow fewer than zero people alive on earth have ever asked a librarian for a business card.

Lukas had my wife's phone one time when he was around 10 years old and I texted him to see if he wanted to go fishing when I got home from work. He replied that he "still had four emails to send" and was too busy to "leave the office."

You'll excuse me if I sit back in wonder at his strange entrepreneurial spirit, even if I've seen it all before. My younger son, Reames, and I are happy to play ball in our tiny librarian's backyard while Lukas makes plans to rule the galaxy. I only wish my dad were here to laugh at the irony and give Lukas tips and encouragement in avenues that I have experience but no interest.

If he were alive today, Dad would be turning 75 this year. If he were alive, Francisco Belman, the boy punched in the heart until it quit responding would be 33. Kimi Slattery, murdered by her husband's boyfriend, would be just 30.

Of course, were he alive today, Joseph Bell, a Scottish surgeon and early pioneer of forensic pathology thought to be the inspiration for Sherlock Holmes would be 183 years old.

The point is, if you grow up living around death you tend to have a perspective of just how short life is and how little time you have to make an impact. Some people think it's morbid, but I guess I'm reassured by the finite start and end dates surrounding existence. That's probably something my dad unknowingly instilled in me and I'd thank him if I could.

Still, there are times when I wonder. Times like when I was helping a friend move from an apartment to a house. Though my friend was younger than I am, he'd asked me to help move furniture and appliances because he knew his dad was too old to be helping without risk of health issues. When we'd gotten his washing machine about halfway up the stairs, he called out.

"Dad, come get this!" he yelled. "Dad! I can't go another step!"

His father came and relieved him, pushing those last five steps with me.

Obviously it wasn't a lot to have to push - even for a 60-year-old - but it struck me that when my friend needed that emergency help, he called on his dad, despite there being others capable of helping in the same room.

I'd not made that call in years. I'll never make it again. But I can say that when I needed it it had been there. He had been there. I've heard it said that with fatherhood quantity time is more important than quality time. He'd managed to give that despite multiple jobs that I didn't want to inherit and a clashing personality.

And just like the example my dad set, my boys can find me when they need me.

I won't be at the morgue.

But you already knew that.

Acknowledgements

This was written during a time of quarantine at the state and local level in an effort to combat the Covid-19 global pandemic. In other words, there wasn't much else to do but stay indoors and dream of better days to come. Part of that meant reaching into the past, and the first acknowledgement goes to my mom, Judy Copeland, for preserving the archives and records related to my dad's long career inside four giant Rubbermaid containers. She helped with the recall of some of these anecdotes, as well.

My wife, Leigh, also encouraged me to turn this loose collection of stories she's heard a thousand times into a book. Often I would write at my dining room table while she sat across from me on her sewing machine. We each had our quarantine activities.

My boys, Lukas and Reames, allowed me the time to write, even if it mostly came after they went to sleep. Keeping them active during the day was my primary job. Writing is always secondary.

My sister also graciously shared her perspective through some of this. She adored my dad and that adoration was mutual. Her stories are through a different lens, even if some of them mirror mine.

A big thank you to my friends Justine and Justin Hardy for being open about their experience and sharing it with me in an attempt to break up my "voice" throughout this book. I hope they don't regret it, because readers definitely needed it.

Finally, my "regular" editor at the Beaufort Gazette retired before quarantine but was called back into action during the pandemic to help cover breaking news. I desperately needed someone to read this, offer suggestions, make corrections, and not ask for too much in return. Cresta Bernhisel, with whom I get the pleasure of working at Battery Creek High School, graciously checked all those marks. She teaches freshman English and there's no one I trust more with grammar oversight. Every edit she suggested not only made the writing better and more readable, she made the corrections in a kind and timely manner. Any mistakes still present in the text are solely my responsibility-she has done her diligence. She's a shining, though sometimes overlooked gem at Battery Creek and I'm grateful for her taking this on.

PRAISE FOR *WAKING UP DEAD*:

"This book is words on a page." - *Manhattan (Kansas) Review*

"How are you going to sell this only online? Are you going to send out an email or something?" - My mother.

"Probably one of the best memoirs written about growing up the son of a funeral director. In the South. Specifically in the coastal area of South Carolina. Beaufort County, especially. In 2020. That good enough?" - My former editor.

"People might read some of this before they turn away in disgust and/or confusion." - *The Lowcountry Ledger*

"The author seems to think death is a joke. He will one day die and I bet he won't find it funny." - *deathisnotfunny.com*

"Destined to be on our bestsellers list!" - *New York Times New Roman Daily Sentinel*

About the author:

 Ryan Copeland, a Beaufort native, is the librarian/media specialist at Battery Creek High School in Beaufort. He has been a regular columnist with the *Beaufort Gazette* and *Island Packet* since 2014. In addition to his column, he is the author of *The Beauty of Beaufort, Hilton Head Island: Discover the Treasures of One of America's Most Cherished Towns* and a contributor to *Along Southern Roads.* He lives in Beaufort with his wife, Leigh and their sons Lukas and Reames.

Made in the USA
Columbia, SC
14 October 2021